The Light in the Swamp

Also by Velda Johnston

THE PHANTOM COTTAGE

I CAME TO A CASTLE

A HOWLING IN THE WOODS

HOUSE ABOVE HOLLYWOOD

ALONG A DARK PATH

The Light in the Swamp

Velda Johnston

A Red Badge Novel of Suspense

DODD, MEAD & COMPANY · NEW YORK

ISBN 0-396-06199-0
Library of Congress Catalog Card Number: 74-121976
Printed in the United States of America
by Vail-Ballou Press, Inc., Binghamton, N.Y.

For Emma Allcock of Evesham, England,
whom many families have felt proud
and privileged to call Nannie

1

Whenever I recall the last stage of my journey to the old Jessup place that August afternoon nearly a year ago, I visualize not only my little girl and myself, driving through the hot stillness of the eastern Long Island woods in a shabby compact car. I also picture the house, that house I'd never seen, awaiting us beyond a few more turns in the narrow private road. I imagine it standing there in the near-sunset light, its scabrous façade speaking of long neglect, but conveying no hint of the malevolence that had settled itself in the high-ceilinged old rooms and airy corridors beyond, where my mother had grown to adulthood.

Even if, by some magic, I'd caught a prevision of that house toward which I drove, it would have made no difference. In my need to find temporary refuge for my child and myself, I'd still have kept moving along the rutted road, between the rows of oaks and maples whose branches, intermingling overhead, shut out every stray breeze.

I drove slowly, fearful that the undercarriage of my little car might catch against the road's humped and weed-grown center. In my grandfather's time, when much of this acreage had been a working farm, the road must have been wider and more well-kept. It was obvious now, though, from the almost unbroken wall of trees on either side, that the land hadn't been farmed for many years.

Beside me on the front seat, Nicole asked, "Where are we going, Mama?"

She knew the answer. It was just that like many five-year-olds, she took a fancy to certain phrases.

"We're going to Nana's old home, and our new home."

Her small body in its blue denim sunsuit wriggled with pleasure. "Nana's old home," she chanted, "and our new home."

I recalled someone's definition of that word: "Home is where, when you go there, they can't throw you out."

Would my Aunt Marian and her husband, Loren Hauklid, want to throw me out? Certainly I'd feared they might try to prevent our coming. That's why I hadn't phoned them from Chicago, or even New York. Instead, from a small Pennsylvania town we'd passed through early that morning, I'd sent them a wire: "Nicole and I arriving sometime this afternoon. Love, Catherine Morrel."

Once we were actually on their doorstep, I'd figured, they wouldn't turn us away. For one thing, they'd have no morally defensible reason to. My mother was now dead. Whatever emotions the thought of her still aroused in the Hauklids—lingering bitterness in my Aunt Marian's breast, longing or guilt in her husband's—surely after all these years those emotions weren't strong enough to make them deny refuge to Nicole and me.

What was more, I had at least some legal right to come here. Despite the signs I'd seen posted for almost a mile along the main road—*Private Lands. No Trespassing. Loren Hauklid, Owner*—despite those signs, neither Aunt Marian nor her husband owned this property. My grandfather, in his righteous wrath, had made sure that neither of those sinners—neither his younger daughter, nor his elder daughter's husband—would ever hold title to one foot of his land or one dollar of his cash estate. True, he'd left my Aunt Marian the use of his land during her lifetime, and the income from his not-too-large cash estate. But after her death, according to the new will he'd made that tumultuous summer thirty years ago, all his estate was to pass to his elder daughter's son, and to any other of his grandchildren who might be born to either of his daughters.

As it turned out, there'd been no other grandchild but myself. And so my Cousin Byron and I would someday be co-owners of these woods, and the old house toward which I drove.

We passed what had once been an apple orchard, most of its trees festooned now with Virginia creeper and poison ivy. Many branches were jaggedly broken, and junipers and young oaks had sprung up in what must once have been well-tended aisles between the trees. Why, I wondered, hadn't the Hauklids continued to farm this land, as they had a right to under the terms of my grandfather's will? It seemed doubly strange when one considered that it was as an agricultural expert, newly graduated from Cornell, that Loren Hauklid had come to eastern Long Island. My grandfather, feeling his years, had hired young Loren to manage these acres—

His years. Maybe one could feel one's years at almost any age. Certainly I was feeling all twenty-six of mine now.

In the car's left windwing, I saw the dim reflection of my face, still pale and thin in its frame of dark blond hair. Suddenly I remembered how, one day the previous fall, I'd gone out to buy vodka for the sixth anniversary party Bill and I were giving. Refusing to believe that I was of age, the liquor store owner had demanded to see my driver's license. Well, he wouldn't demand that now.

"Stop it!" I told myself. Self-pity was a luxury for the well-heeled. I couldn't afford to waste energy feeling sorry for myself. In the French-made calfskin handbag, Bill's gift last Christmas, which lay on the seat between Nicole and me, was all the money I had in the world—ninety-one dollars and some small change.

Again I glanced at my pale reflection in the windwing. Well, out here in the clean air and sunlight of eastern Long Island, I'd soon gain back the color and weight I'd lost. And surely right now I could hold down at least a part-time job, leaving Nicole in Aunt Marian's care. I wouldn't impose upon the Hauklids any longer than necessary. As soon as I was fit again, and had built up a small nest egg, Nicole and I would go back to Chicago.

Ahead, on the left-hand side of the road, was a break in the trees. I drove even more slowly as I passed it, looking at the rectangular plot with its twenty or so worn gravestones, enclosed by a waist-high railing. This, I knew, must be the Jessups' private cemetery, where for almost a century and a half my mother's people had been buried.

A few yards farther on I stopped at the roadside. "Wait here a moment, darling." Walking back along the road, dappled with leaf shadow and the brassy sunlight of late afternoon, I unlatched the little gate. The latch was unrusted, and the railing looked as if it had been repainted not too long ago. No matter how the Hauklids neglected the rest of this property, they'd given adequate care to the family graveyard. I relatched the gate behind me, turned, and felt the startled leap of the pulse in the hollow of my throat.

A dark-haired man stood motionless in the far corner of the little cemetery.

We stared at each other through the hot stillness. Had

he been here when I drove past only seconds ago? Undoubtedly. But he couldn't have been standing then, or I would have seen him. He must have been crouching behind that tall gravestone, a foot or so from where he now stood.

Was he Byron? He appeared to be about the right age, somewhere in his early thirties. But no, he wasn't that poor, flawed cousin I'd never seen. This man's eyes, gray in a tanned, high-cheekboned face, held intelligent alertness. Something else, too. Guilt? Fear?

Could he have been *hiding* behind that gravestone? Perhaps he'd heard my car, and dropped down, thinking I'd drive on past—

Whether he felt fear or not, I was aware of ripples of alarm down my own body. Everything was so quiet. Here in the heat-smothered woods, not even the birds sang. Except for Nicole, there probably wasn't another human being within sound of my voice. And at the very best, this man was a knowing trespasser. No one could have missed those signs that Loren Hauklid had posted every few yards along the main highway.

Uneasiness sharpened my voice. "Who are you? What are you doing here?"

If there had been alarm in his eyes, it had gone now, leaving his gaze cool and steady. He said, with a slight smile, "No fair. The first trespasser, not the second, gets to ask that question."

Annoyance rose through my alarm. "I'm not a trespasser at all. I'm the Hauklids' niece."

He seemed to tense. "Loren Hauklid's niece?"

"Mrs. Hauklid's. Now will you please tell me who you are?"

He was smiling again. "Of course. My name's Philip Owen. I've been teaching summer school at Southampton College. And I have an appointment to teach a course called Aspects of American Civilization, starting in the fall."

Was that true? His clothing—thick-soled shoes, chinos, and a blue pullover—didn't look very professional. But "Aspects of American Civilization" had an authentic academic ring. And his voice, touched with an accent I couldn't define, was that of an educated man.

I relaxed somewhat. "Didn't you see those no-trespassing signs?"

"Who could miss them? But I thought they'd been posted to keep out hunters and campers. I didn't see how someone with an antiquarian interest in old graveyards could do any harm."

"I suppose you're right." Unwilling to sound stuffy, I didn't add that he might have phoned to get the Hauklids' permission before invading a private burial ground.

"Have you been staying with your aunt and uncle quite awhile?"

"I haven't stayed with them at all. I mean, I've never met them. I'm on my way to their house now."

"Then you're not from around here?"

"No, Chicago."

A small hand slipped into mine. Nicole had walked under the railing, and now stood staring at Philip Owen.

He smiled at her. But that indicated nothing about him. Even people who dislike children often break into a startled smile at sight of that silky, lemon-yellow hair, that little face set with what I think of as brook-brown eyes. They're the same shade, and have the same clarity, as brook water flowing over a bed of brown leaves.

"Daughter? Kid sister?"

That last probably had been sheer, outrageous flattery. But after that depressing reflection I'd caught in the car's windwing only minutes before, I found it pleasant. "Daughter."

"You and your husband are lucky."

I hesitated, and then said, "My husband is dead."

"Oh! I'm sorry." The gray eyes, as they went from my face to Nicole's and then back again, did seem to hold a certain compassion.

"Well," he said, after a moment, "I'll leave you now and get back to my car. I left it parked over on the highway." Turning, he lifted a hook I hadn't noticed before. He raised a hinged section of the railing, stepped out of the graveyard, and then turned back to refasten the hook. "Good-by for now, Mrs.—?"

"Morrel, Catherine Morrel. And this is Nicole."

He smiled. "Well, good-by to both of you." Turning, he walked away through the trees.

2

Nicole asked, "Who was that man, Mama?"

"Just a man. He teaches in a college near here."

She was looking around her, small face awed and a bit frightened. "Where—where are we?"

"This is a graveyard, darling. Will you go back to the car and wait for me? I'll be only a minute or two."

Already, poor mite, she'd become acquainted with death. Someday soon I'd bring her back here, and tell her what I knew of those men and women, ancestors of hers, who slept in this quiet place. But right now I was too tired for more than a cursory tour of the little cemetery.

Obediently she trotted off. I stepped closer to the nearest and newest-looking gravestone. It read: "Samuel Jessup, 1870–1940."

Samuel Jessup, my grandfather, who'd turned my mother out of the house where she was born. As I thought of the huge Chicago cemetery in which she now lay, my still-raw grief for her stirred. Here was where she belonged. If the authorities still permitted burial in small family cemeteries, I'd have her casket brought here, just as soon as I had a little spare money. I'd need the Hauklids' permission, of course, but surely they'd give it.

I glanced at other gravestones. Howard Jessup, 1844–1903. My great-grandfather. Martha Harkness Jessup, his wife, 1850–1916. Amy Jessup, 1839–1932. She must have been that enormously aged great-aunt whom my mother had remembered from her own childhood. Here were three little graves—Edith, John, and Matthew Jessup—who'd died in 1852 at the ages of eight, seven, and four. Typhoid, I thought, or smallpox, or one of those other diseases that used to wipe out whole families.

I moved to the oldest of the gravestones, the one beside which Philip Owen had stood. The lettering was so worn I could scarcely make it out: Jethro Jessup, 1767–1852. My great-great-great-grandfather. Beside him lay his three wives—Charity, who was probably the first one, on his right, and Martha and Abigail on his left. All three had died before the age of forty. Well, life was hard on women in the days when wives not only cooked and scrubbed, but made their own soap and candles, wove their own cloth, and, occasionally, caught an Indian arrow in the back. As to which of those three wives was my own ancestress, I had no idea.

Again I looked at Jethro Jessup's grave. It was not only the oldest in the little cemetery. It was by far the longest. I recalled my mother mentioning that Jethro's height of six-feet-four had been a legend in the family.

Leaving the graveyard, I returned to the car. My travel-weary little daughter had fallen asleep, curled up in the corner of the seat, her lashes lying like silky brown fans on her flushed cheeks. She didn't wake up as I got quietly into the car and drove off down the narrow, winding road. It was almost sunset now. The light filtering through the trees had taken on a reddish color.

A few minutes later I drove onto the bare, hard-packed

earth of a large clearing, stopped the car—and stared in dismay. Could this be the Jessup house? Yes, there was the three-story original structure my mother had described to me, and the wings of two stories each which had been added by my great-great grandfather. But the once-white clapboards were yellowed and peeling now.

And where was the wide lawn, set with fruit trees, that my mother had told me about? One apple tree remained, its branches hung with speckled and misshapen fruit. But except for a few tufts of coarse grass here and there, the lawn had vanished.

Just then I learned why. From around the corner of the house strolled five white leghorn hens and a rooster, bobbing their red-combed heads and clucking. One of the hens stopped, scratched at the dirt, and seized some goody, probably a worm, in her beak. With the other fowls in squawking pursuit, she ran back around the corner of the house.

So the Hauklids had sacrificed a once-beautiful lawn to keep chickens. Why? Well, if they were living off the income from my grandfather's estate, they were poor—poor enough that they would need a cheap source of meat and eggs. But why did they have to be that poor? Why didn't Loren Hauklid farm these many acres? And even if for some unguessable reason he'd lost interest in farming, surely he'd have been able to find other employment in one of the prosperous-looking villages and towns I'd passed through that afternoon.

Perhaps he suffered from some chronic illness. But if so, my Aunt Marian had never mentioned it in any of her infrequent letters to my mother.

Nicole stirred, opened her eyes, and stared at the house. I watched the blinking confusion in her little face turn to dismay. She said, almost with a whimper, "Mama, is this our new home?"

"Yes, but we won't be here long."

"I don't like it."

"I know, darling. But it will be all right for a while. Now will you wait just a minute?"

I got out of the car and then turned to close the door. It didn't latch properly. Even when the car was new, its door latches sometimes failed to hold, and they hadn't improved in the four years since. Drawing the door back, I slammed it shut.

The sound triggered an explosion of barks and snarls. At least two dogs, somewhere nearby, were making that uproar. Nicole let out a terrified wail.

Slipping back into the car, I said quickly, "They won't hurt us." But I wasn't sure of that. These didn't sound like the usual family pets, expressing a belligerence as false as it was noisy. Their snarls seemed to hold a real threat. Swiftly I cranked up the window on Nicole's side, and then on mine. The dogs still barked and snarled, but the sound had come no closer. That must mean that they were tied up, or penned. Still, I'd take no chances. I'd wait until the Hauklids came out.

Why hadn't they come out? Surely by now, if only because of the dogs' barking, they must be aware that someone had arrived.

A tall man in blue denim shirt and trousers came walking around the corner of the house from where the white leghorns had appeared. He was bouncing a red rubber ball. With the car windows closed, and the dogs making that racket, I couldn't hear his voice. But from the movement of his lips I guessed that he was counting. "One, two, three, four; one, two, three, four—"

My Cousin Byron, surely.

Rolling down the car window, I called, "Hello!"

He caught the ball in his two hands, looked up. For a moment he stared at me with what seemed pleased surprise. Then he came toward the car with an odd, loping gait.

I felt a stab of pity for the aunt I'd never met. Byron, she'd christened her infant son. Surely her choice of name must have been an indication of what she'd hoped he'd become—handsome, distinguished, perhaps even famous. Well, in at least one respect her hopes had been fulfilled. Now that he stood beside the car, I saw how very good-looking he was. Lustrous, light brown hair, one lock falling over the unlined forehead. Even features, and eyes that were large and gray and serene. In a child's face, such eyes would have been beautiful. But my cousin was six years older than I, and so the artless friendliness of his gaze filled me with dismayed compassion.

"Hello," he said. His gaze went past me to Nicole, and his smile widened.

"Are those dogs vicious?" Seeing the blankness in the eyes he turned toward me, I amended, "Do your dogs bite?"

"Sure." His tone was proud. "Old King and Prince are plenty mean."

"Are they loose now?"

"They're in their cage. Come on. I'll show you."

Getting out of the car, I lifted Nicole down to the hard-packed earth. She walked between us as we moved across the yard. "Where are your father and mother?"

"They drove to Neptague right after lunch."

Neptague was the nearest village. I'd driven through it not forty minutes ago. "Didn't they get my telegram? I mean, didn't someone bring a yellow envelope, or perhaps telephone?"

"Sure. Old Jimmy brought it."

Old Jimmy. Probably the sort of man who, in rural communities, ekes out a livelihood by delivering telegrams and special delivery letters, doing yard work, and providing taxi service.

"Are you sure the envelope was yellow?"

"Sure. And Mama said it was from Catherine."

So they knew I was coming, and yet they'd left. I'd steeled myself for a cool reception. What I hadn't anticipated was no reception at all.

He asked, "Are you Catherine?"

"Yes, and I know you're Byron. And this is Nicole."

"Hello," my daughter said. "Could I hold that ball?" Usually a little standoffish with grownups, she'd spoken calmly and directly, as if to a contemporary. Some instinct had told her that the friendly, gangling creature beside us was not a man, but a child.

"Sure," he said, and transferred the red ball from one of his big hands to her two small ones.

As we drew nearer to the dogs, their snarls and barks took on a hysterical note. We rounded the corner of the house and there they were, two Dobermans, sleek bundles of fury penned by steel-mesh fencing on three sides, and on the fourth by the house's peeling clapboards. Reddish sunlight rippled along their dark coats as they leapt, snarling, at the ten-foot fence, fell back, leapt again.

"King! Prince! Shut up!" my cousin said. Instantly the barking ceased. They began to pace the bare earth, ears flattened, narrow heads turning to watch us.

Byron was looking at me proudly. "Thanks," I said. "Are the dogs ever turned loose?"

"Sometimes Papa lets them out."

My gaze on the pacing animals, I shuddered. Strange, I thought. Here were these signs of near-poverty—peeling paint, and chickens scratching in the bare farmyard. And yet here were two thoroughbred and obviously well-nourished dogs, penned behind expensive steel fencing. Surely it was Loren Hauklid who'd bought the dogs. And almost as surely my Aunt Marian, watching her family home decay, must resent the money he spent on these animals.

What sort of man was he, anyway? Or rather, what sort of man had he become? Because perhaps he'd changed since that long-ago summer when the young girl who'd become my mother fell in love with him. Again I seemed to hear her voice, speaking reluctantly and painfully from the high hospital bed. "It wasn't just that he was handsome, although he was, like—like a young Viking. He was so gentle, Catherine. And no matter what happened, he was a *good* man."

Nicole had begun to bounce the ball, catching it in both hands. Byron watched her, obviously delighted with her delight in the plaything he'd loaned her. I said, "Did your parents tell you what room we were to have?" He looked at me blankly. "Did they say where we were to sleep?"

His face lit up. "I remember." He turned and, with his loping gait, led us back around the corner of the house. Climbing three steps to the small roofless front porch, he pulled back the screen door. The door beyond it stood open. As I walked into this house I'd never seen until today, I suddenly wondered how often my mother had returned here in her dreams, stepping with young-girl lightness from the lush and tree-shadowed lawn, crossing the little porch, moving into the lower hall with its grandfather's clock, its Aubusson floor runner that had been brought over by clipper ship in 1850—

There in the hall's dimness, I stopped short. The clock still stood against the wall, majestically ticking. But the Aubusson runner was gone. It had been replaced by brown linoleum, now cracked and worn thin in spots. I stared at it, feeling depressed. Only people who'd given up caring where or how they lived could have replaced an heirloom, treasured by four generations of Jessups, with that linoleum.

I glanced through a doorway at my right. The dining room. At least it still held the Chinese Chippendale table my mother had described. To my left was what even in my mother's childhood had still been called the parlor. I gained an impression of an odd mixture of furniture sitting there in the hot dimness—a nice old marble-topped table and a Victorian sofa, a fairly new black plastic-covered armchair, and a television set on a rollaway stand.

"Come on!" Byron called. Halfway up the staircase that rose through the shadows at the rear of the hall, he'd stopped to look back at us.

"We're coming." As I climbed the stairs, with Nicole holding to my hand, I saw that the hand-hooked stair runner my mother had told me about was still there. Each riser bore the state flower of one of the thirteen original states, and each tread the seal of one of those states. The runner had been made during her young womanhood by Amy Jessup, that extremely aged spinster who'd still been alive when my mother was a girl.

On the landing Byron turned into a long, dim hallway leading along the north wing. At its end I could see, by the light of a tall window, a flight of stairs leading down. I recalled my mother telling me that each wing of the house had its own stairs leading to the first floor.

Byron stopped at the second door on the right. "Here it is."

The room was pleasant enough. A worn Axminster rug. A double mahogany bed, with a crocheted coverlet, and a matching chest of drawers. From somewhere—the attic, probably—the Hauklids had brought in a child's railed bed of white metal, its paint chipped in spots.

Across the room, and a foot or so out from the wall, a full-length oval mirror hung on swivels in its footed mahogany frame. Walking to it, I looked at my reflection. I was so pale. Even if I found a job right away, I hoped Nicole and I could spend an hour or so at the beach in the late afternoon.

Lost in my own thoughts, I was unaware that Byron had moved around behind the mirror until he poked that strangely young face of his around the mahogany frame. I gave a startled exclamation. He said in that still, remote voice children use when speaking of something that frightens them, "I remember it. The one in the mirror shot the other one. There was blood on the floor and the wall."

I stared at him through the fading light that came through a nearby window. It seemed to me that the luminous gray eyes had darkened, and the unlined face had become taut.

"Byron! What on earth—!" Then I softened my tone. "So you make up stories. That's all right. But why not make up nice ones?"

"It's not a story!" His voice held rising excitement. "The one in the mirror had a gun, and the other one—"

In the glass I could see Nicole standing rigid just inside the doorway, staring at Byron with wide, frightened eyes. I said swiftly, "Byron, will you go downstairs and get my suitcase? It's in the trunk of my car. You can do that for me, can't you?"

The excitement in his face gave way to momentary bewilderment. Then he said proudly, "You bet."

I waited until I heard him clattering down the stairs. Then I crossed the room to Nicole. "Let's find the bathroom, darling."

She didn't move. "Mama, I don't like our new home. Do we have to stay here?"

Kneeling, I drew her close. "Yes, darling. I can't explain, but we do have to stay here, for at least a little while. It won't be so bad. We'll go to the beach, and for walks in the woods—"

Through the open window came the sound of a car driving into the yard. Swiftly I crossed the room and looked down.

A man and a woman I knew must be the Hauklids were getting out of a worn black sedan.

3

After turning on the beside lamp and telling Nicole to wait for me, I hurried out of the room and down the stairs. When I emerged onto the little front porch, Loren Hauklid was taking my suitcase from my car. Byron stood at his elbow, chattering excitedly. My aunt, clutching the frame of a shabby black purse with both hands, stood watching.

I called, with self-conscious brightness, "Hello, there!"

They turned. After a second's pause, the woman waved, and the three of them started toward me. As I moved off the porch to meet them, I was aware of the reversal in our roles—I emerging hostess-like from the house, they advancing like newly arrived guests.

We met almost in the center of the ugly yard. Marian Hauklid wore the same forced smile I felt on my own lips. Would they want me to call them aunt and uncle, or by their first names? Not knowing, I merely said, "I'm Catherine."

"Hello, Catherine." Her voice, like her face, was tense. "I'm your Aunt Marian, and this is your Uncle Loren." Leaning forward, she kissed me. After a moment her husband set down the suitcase and, bending, brushed his lips across my cheek.

A young Viking, my mother had said. He was no longer young, but the Viking look remained—in his more than six feet of height, and his graying but still thick blond hair, and his strong-featured face set with blue eyes as dark as the sea on a clear winter's day.

Apparently feeling she could handle these first awkward moments better if she and I were alone, my aunt said, "Loren, why don't you and Byron take Catherine's suitcase upstairs?" As he picked up the suitcase, I noticed that the little finger on his left hand must have sustained some injury in the past. It was bent so that it projected outward from his otherwise normal hand. I watched him move toward the house, with Byron loping ahead. What a tragic mockery, I thought, this son who resembled him so—until you saw that Byron's thirty-two years had left almost no weight of experience in his eyes.

My aunt said, as we moved slowly toward the house, "I'm sorry we were out when you got here. But you see—well, we went to the village to find—nicer accommodations for you and the little girl. We'd have paid for them, of course."

She gave a nervous laugh and then went on, "The trouble was, the few places vacant were just out of the question. The Hamptons have always been expensive in the summertime, but I hadn't realized just how high prices are now. Two hundred dollars a week for a motel room—and in advance! Why, the very best motels out here used to charge only six dollars a day."

Shock held me silent. They'd so disliked the idea of our staying here that they'd been willing to subsidize other lodgings for Nicole and me. Probably if they'd had the two hundred dollars with them—

She laid her hand on my arm. The nervous abruptness

of the gesture made me almost certain she'd read my thoughts. "Let's sit in the living room for a minute and get acquainted."

"All right," I said woodenly. As we stepped into the lower hall, now deep in shadow, I added, "Perhaps I'd better see Nicole for a moment before we talk."

Upstairs I found my suitcase in our room, but no sign of the male Hauklids. Perhaps they'd moved along the second-floor hallway to the other wing. I settled Nicole on the big bed, and gave her a picture book from the suitcase.

When I went down to the living room, I found that my aunt had turned on a lamp, a lovely old pewter one that probably a hundred years ago had been fueled by whale oil. Now its electric glow fell on my aunt's graying brown hair as she sat beside it, smiling nervously, on the small Victorian sofa. The sofa's needlepoint upholstery, I noticed, was badly worn. As I started to sit down in the black plastic armchair, she said quickly, "Not that chair. It's Loren's TV chair. You know how men are about their chairs."

I didn't. Bill had never been any particular way about chairs, nor had any other man I'd known. But I gave a noncommittal nod and sat down at the other end of the sofa. She clasped her hands tightly in her lap and leaned toward me.

"Catherine, please don't be hurt because we tried to find another place for you. It's just that this is no place for a young girl, a shabby house stuck away off here in the woods."

My tone was dry. "I'd scarcely describe myself as a teenybopper."

"But you are young. And you're pretty," she added. "You look like your mother."

So did she, at least enough so that one might have guessed that she and my mother had been sisters. But unlike Mother, who'd kept much of her looks up until those last weeks before her death, Marian Hauklid wasn't pretty. Even in early snapshots I'd seen, her face, although gentle and appealing, had been no match for my mother's. Aunt Marian's nose was a shade too prominent, and her chin not quite enough so. But it was the unhappy lines around her mouth, and the anxious, even frightened look in her light blue eyes, which robbed her of any claim to attractiveness.

That unhappiness wasn't just in her. Increasingly I was aware of unhappiness in the very atmosphere of this old house. What caused it? Their son's failure to develop mentally? But surely they should have adjusted to that by now. Their poverty? But I could think of no reason why they should be as poor as they seemed to be. Was it the memory of that old entanglement between Loren Hauklid and my mother which poisoned the very air of this house? But that had happened long, long ago.

I said, "Please try to understand. I had to come here. In my purse upstairs I have less than a hundred dollars. And that's all the cash I have in the world."

After a moment she asked, "Didn't Bill leave any insurance?" From the look in her eyes, I knew she'd been ashamed to ask that question, and yet had felt she had to.

"He cashed it in about eight months before his death, and used the money to start his own advertising agency." ("Darling," he'd said, "as soon as the agency gets rolling, I'm going to take out a whacking big policy for you and the Nuisance. But the best way now to insure our future is for me to start my own business. Besides, we don't need insurance. I'm still young and healthy." What had not occurred to either of us was that even the healthiest man might not survive a three-car smashup.)

She said, "Couldn't Bill's people have helped you?"

Oh, how she must want to get rid of me! The impulse to leave this house was almost overwhelming. But I couldn't give in to it. Upstairs I'd left, turning the pages of her picture book, my little hostage to fortune.

"Bill's parents are quite old now. They were almost middle-aged when they married. Ten years ago they used what little money they had to buy into one of those retirement villages. Their only income is social security. Bill does have an older brother in Chicago, but he's trying to support a wife and four children on a bookkeeper's salary. I couldn't add Nicole and myself to his burdens."

"I—I see."

"I didn't mention it in my wire, so you had no way of knowing. But I'd have been able to get by on my own if I hadn't fallen ill recently. It was pneumonia."

Perhaps one's strength lasts as long as it has to. Mine had lasted for almost seven months after Bill's death. I'd taken an office job with the same advertising firm that once had employed him. Each afternoon I'd collected Nicole from the private kindergarten where I'd placed her, and then returned to the apartment to cook dinner for the two of us. After dinner I'd take Nicole to the hospital and leave her under the watchful eyes of the nurses at the reception desk while I sat beside my mother's bed. When visiting hours were over, I'd take Nicole home, put her to bed, finish my housework, and do whatever was necessary —washing underthings, manicuring my nails, setting my hair—to get ready for the office the next day. Sometime around midnight or one, I'd set the alarm for six-thirty, and fall into bed.

Except for the nagging cough I'd developed, I felt I was holding up nicely. But the morning after my mother's funeral I awoke with my body on fire and an invisible steel band tightening around my chest. Somehow I got to the phone and called my doctor. He put me in the hospital for three weeks.

The afternoon I emerged, weak and shaky, from the

hospital, I collected Nicole from the kindly upstairs neighbor, a middle-aged widow, who'd cared for her in my absence. Then, in the silent living room of my apartment, I sat down and jotted figures on the back of an old envelope.

My mother's unpaid funeral expenses. My entire hospital bill, and the fairly small amount still owing on my mother's. One month's overdue rent and utility bills. Nicole's kindergarten fees. And the amount I was determined to pay my neighbor for her care of Nicole. I added all these figures, and subtracted their sum from what was left in the savings account Bill and I had held jointly.

The result was two hundred and eleven dollars and thirty-two cents. I added and subtracted again, hoping the answer would be different. It wasn't.

In growing panic, I stared down at those figures. My doctor had forbidden me to work full-time for at least another month. Even if I risked disobeying him, my salary wouldn't pay for food and the rent of this fairly expensive apartment and Nicole's kindergarten. All along I'd been dipping into savings to meet those expenses. I'd need some cheaper arrangement for her daytime care, and a cheaper apartment. But even if I managed to find such an apartment, moving our furniture would cost several hundred dollars.

A salary loan? A loan on the furniture? No, no! Even couples who turned to loan companies often found themselves spiraling deeper and deeper into debt. For me, with my limited experience in financial matters, such a course might lead to complete disaster.

It was then that I'd thought of my grandfather's house on eastern Long Island.

No longer despairing, I again jotted figures on the envelope. There was no need to put down anything for the storage of my furniture. You didn't pay such bills, I'd heard, until you took your furniture out. But it would cost money to get Nicole and me to Long Island. After several moments I gave a relieved sigh. Yes, even after I'd paid my debts, there'd still be enough money for gasoline, and for food and lodging along the road—

Now I said to my aunt, "I need to get back on my feet, in every way. And I had nowhere else to turn. You and Nicole are the only blood relatives I have, except for those second cousins of yours and Mother's out in—Utah?"

"Wyoming. Well, I guess you'd better stay here." She sounded almost relieved, as if knowing there was no help for it had resolved, however unsatisfactorily, some torturing dilemma.

"We won't be here long, not more than a few months. I feel well enough right now to hold down some light job. After I'm strong again, and have saved a few hundred dollars—"

"You shouldn't have any trouble finding a job in one of the villages around here."

"I suppose I'd make money fastest by waiting table in one of those expensive restaurants I've heard about, but it might be too strenuous. I'd better stick to office work."

"Yes, that would be safer."

"I'll pay board, of course."

"Oh, no!" she said hastily. "There's no reason to. The room's there anyway. And what little food you and Nicole will eat—" She broke off, and then said, in a low voice, "Tell me about your mother."

I knew what she meant. She wanted to know more about my mother's death.

"Well, as usual she came from Philadelphia to Chicago to spend last Christmas with Bill and Nicole and me." I paused, and then said, "I guess you knew that after I married Bill and went to Chicago, Mother moved in with a Philadelphia friend, Grace Halliday."

"Certainly I knew it." My aunt's voice was a trifle stiff.

"Your mother and I didn't correspond frequently, but we always wrote to each other at Christmas. I knew she was living with a Mrs. Halliday."

"Well, I wasn't sure. Anyway, the day Mother was to fly back to Philadelphia, Nicole woke up with a cold, so I stayed home while Bill drove Mother to the airport. The road was icy, and there was a three-car crash—"

My throat closed, making speech impossible. When I was able to, I went on, "Bill died instantly. Mother was terribly injured. After five months in the hospital, she died on the operating table. They were trying to reset a thighbone that hadn't knitted properly, but she was too weak to withstand the surgical shock."

My aunt's lips shook. Turning her head away, she said in a low voice, "Poor little Caroline, poor little sister."

I felt sudden rage. I wanted to say, "But you didn't come to see your little sister, did you, even though I wired you she was in the hospital. You didn't even come to her funeral."

Then I felt ashamed of myself. There'd been genuine grief in her voice. I could imagine no reason why she'd remained away from my mother, but that didn't mean that there couldn't have been a reason, and a compelling one.

She turned back to me, "Catherine, I'm sorry to have seemed so—uncordial. But I didn't feel you'd find it pleasant here, and besides, I—we—we're so used to being by ourselves."

"That's all right. It's only natural that you'd find it disconcerting to have me descend out of the blue."

I didn't think it was natural, not when I was her niece, and not when she knew of my double bereavement. I didn't think that anything about her behavior was natural, nor about the atmosphere of this house. But beggars, I reminded myself with more grimness than originality, can't be choosers.

"I'll be as little trouble as possible. For instance, I imagine it would be more convenient for you if I gave Nicole her supper separately." I glanced at my watch. "Maybe I'd better do that now. And then I can help you with dinner for the rest of us."

She nodded. I was glad she hadn't refused my offer. It was going to be hard enough to be an unwelcome guest, let alone a non-working one.

"But there's no hurry about dinner. We have it late in the summertime. Loren likes to work as long as possible in his vegetable garden after the day starts to cool off."

A vegetable garden. He had a degree in agriculture from Cornell. He'd once managed a successful farming operation on this property. And now he confined himself to working in his vegetable garden.

What was it, I wondered, that had broken the mainspring of the Hauklids' lives?

I rose. "Well, I'll go get Nicole."

4

During the next hour or so, my daughter seemed to lose the uneasiness that had beset her earlier. For one thing, she was impressed by the enormous bathroom in the north wing—one of the three installed before the First World War by my grandfather, Aunt Marian told me—and especially by the wood-enclosed tub in which I gave her a quick pre-supper bath. Too, she fell instantly in love with the Raggedy Ann doll my aunt unearthed from a chest of toys she and my mother had played with as children. And she seemed pleased with her meal of stewed chicken and string beans in the big old kitchen. (The chicken, I knew, must have been a relative of the ones I'd seen in the yard that afternoon. I hoped that neither Nicole nor I would witness the guillotining of the next one.)

Afterwards, while my aunt and I prepared additional vegetables—corn and zucchini, fresh from the garden—Nicole and Byron played outside the kitchen windows in the last of the twilight, tossing the big red ball back and forth. As I watched them, the five-year-old child and the thirty-two-year-old one, something chill stirred in my heart.

Mentally he was about Nicole's age. But what if in other ways—?

The thought must have shown in my face, because my aunt, standing beside me at the sink, said sorrowfully, "You have nothing to worry about. My son is a young child in every way. He's never harmed anyone, and never will."

I looked at her and then quickly away, not wanting her to read pity in my eyes. "Besides," she said, "whenever you're not here, I'll keep watch over her as carefully as if she were my own."

"I know you will."

For a moment there seemed to be a closeness between us, almost as if I'd grown up seeing my aunt at intervals, rather than meeting her for the first time only a few hours before.

But when, with Nicole in bed, I sat down at the old dining room table with the three Hauklids, my sense of strain returned. It wasn't because of Byron's presence. (I'd feared his table manners might be bad, but the proud, careful way he unfolded his paper napkin and spread it on his lap told me he'd been well-trained in that respect.) Rather, it was a tension in the very air. "We're so used to being by ourselves," my aunt had said. Would the presence of any additional person have brought this strain into the atmosphere? Or was it my specific presence that caused it?

After a few moments of uncomfortable silence, Loren Hauklid began to question me about our trip from Chicago. I made my replies. Yes, the weather had been good all the way. No, I'd had no engine trouble.

For a while after that we ate in silence. Finally, to break the strain, I said, "These vegetables are so marvelous. You can tell they were raised by an expert."

Instantly I regretted my words. They'd sounded like a

snide comment on the long-neglected apple orchard I'd passed that afternoon, and the stretches of woodland which must once have been fields of corn or potatoes or cauliflower.

The dark blue eyes in the handsome face looked steadily into mine. "Yes, I like growing things. I only regret that large-scale farming on this land isn't practical any longer. The land needs irrigation. And the water table is so low now that we'd have to sink a number of deep wells. That would cost a small fortune."

"Oh," I said, "I didn't know."

"But we get by. We raise and can a lot of food, and Marian trades chickens and eggs for all sorts of things at the general store in Neptague."

Faint color stained my aunt's cheekbones. Surely she must be thinking the same thing I was. None of the Jessups had ever been actually rich, but they had been, in my mother's phrase, "comfortably off." Surely it had been a long time since anyone of Jessup blood had needed to barter.

"Besides," he went on, "there's Marian's income, and the little business I've worked up."

Marian's income. That income which must seem doubly inadequate whenever they reflected that, if it hadn't been for his moral outrage, my grandfather would have left half his entire estate to them. Feeling embarrassed warmth in my own face now, I asked, "What sort of business?"

"Ceramics. I make them. After dinner I'll show you my workshop, if you want to see it."

"I'd like to very much."

The meal ended soon after that. Loren and his son crossed to the living room. My aunt and I cleared the table and, in the kitchen, began to wash the dishes. For a while some of the strained atmosphere seemed to have followed us from the dining room, but as we worked, she washing and I drying, we began to talk more naturally. I asked her what had become of the Aubusson hall runner my mother had told me about.

"There were holes worn in several places."

"Couldn't it have been mended? I've heard of fine old rugs being rewoven."

After a long moment she said, "It would have been too expensive."

I said quickly, "Well, you still have some beautiful pieces. That dining table, for instance." I thought of the silver-plated knives and forks which, along with chipped but once-valuable china, we'd used at dinner. Perhaps she kept the good flatware stored away. "Do you still have that Samuel Kirk sterling? My mother said it was beautiful."

"No, I sold it. That's when I was still taking Byron to specialists, hoping that—" She broke off, and then said in a sharpened tone, "The silver wasn't part of your grandfather's estate. It was our mother's, Caroline's and mine. When she died—oh, fifteen years before your grandfather did—she left the silver to me, as the elder daughter."

I said, appalled, "Oh, I didn't mean—"

"I know you didn't," she said quickly. After a moment she added, in an odd, jerky voice, "Catherine, whatever—I mean, I want you to know that I think you're a very nice girl."

I said, touched, "Thank you for saying so. And I like you, too." I meant it. Despite her strangeness, despite her obvious unwillingness to have me stay here, she struck a chord of sympathy in me.

We were putting the last of the dishes in the cupboard when Loren appeared in the kitchen doorway. "Want to see my workshop now, Cathy?"

"Why, yes."

Whipping off her apron, my aunt hung it on a hook beside the sink. "I'll go with you."

There'd been increased tension in her voice. I looked at her wonderingly. Could she possibly be jealous of me, the girl whose mother her husband had once been in love with? No, hers wasn't the tight-lipped, glinting-eyed face of an embattled wife. Her obvious anxiety not to let me be alone with him must have some other cause.

Her husband said, after a moment, "All right. Come on."

We moved through the kitchen doorway and out into the hall. As we passed the living room, I looked in and saw Byron, hunched on a worn leather hassock before the television set. On the screen a bay horse with its white-Stetsoned rider was sliding, forefeet braced, down a rock-strewn hillside.

We stepped out into a warm night clamorous with katydids and tree frogs. The watery gleam of a few major stars shone through the thin overcast. Among the trees walling the other side of the farmyard, additional stars seemed to drift green-white for a second or so, and then vanish. Fireflies.

As we rounded the corner of the house, one of the Dobermans, catching my unfamiliar scent mingled with that of the Hauklids', made a sound deep in his throat. Otherwise both the dark, recumbent shapes inside the steel-mesh cage remained silent. We continued past the kennel to a low outbuilding. Half of it served as an open-fronted garage. I could see the dull gleam of the old sedan's rear bumper. Loren led us to the partially open door of the other half, reached inside, and switched on a ceiling light.

We stepped into a bare, meticulously clean little room. In one corner stood a small brick kiln. Arranged in groups on a long table in the center of the room were several dozen little objects of painted ceramic. Football players about three inches high, each grasping a football in his upraised right hand. Miniature church bells. Storks. Little top hats, painted bright green.

He said, "They're place cards for special-occasion dinners. I carve the molds, then fire the clay in that kiln over there, and then paint the pieces. A novelty company in New Jersey buys them."

He picked up a church bell. "For an engagement party. The place card goes in this slit at the top. The storks are for a baby shower, of course, and the green hats for St. Patrick's Day." He set down the bell and picked up a football player. "This is my latest. I designed it last week and turned the first batch out yesterday. It's for a celebration after a big game."

I made an appreciative—and insincere— murmur. To me, the little ceramics had an appalling cuteness. Nor could their manufacture be very profitable. Surely people wouldn't pay much for gadgets they might use only once, or at most a few times. Why should this still-vigorous-looking man spend his days making them?

As if reading my thoughts, he said, "It doesn't pay a great deal, but at least it's better than working for someone else."

So perhaps that was it. Denied the precarious independence of a farmer, he'd turned to work which at least enabled him to call his time his own.

Out in the wire cage, one of the Dobermans barked. Loren said, setting down the football player, "Stop that, King!"

Instantly the dog fell silent. I asked, "Did Byron name them?"

"The Dobermans? No, I did."

What sort of grown man named his dogs King and Prince? A man of almost no imagination? One with a satirical sense of humor? Someone with a secret hankering after some sort of életism?

I said, "Byron told me the dogs can be—dangerous."

He said dryly, "They can."

My aunt spoke for the first time since we left the house. "But they're not loose very often." I knew that her taut little smile was meant to be reassuring.

Her husband said, "Maybe you wonder why I keep them." His face darkened. "It's because this whole country's going to hell. Yes, even out here. Any house that's left unguarded is apt to get broken into. They steal radios, TV sets, tools—anything they can sell to buy liquor or drugs. It's kids doing it, mainly. The whole damn lot of them are degenerate. Oh, not all of them," he added quickly. "I don't mean the few young people like you."

Too dismayed to speak, I nodded acknowledgment of his last words. I was glad my mother couldn't hear that savage outburst from a man who'd lingered in her memory as "gentle." Despite her troubles, she herself had never become embittered, nor browned-off at the new generation, or at anything else in life.

I had a swift memory of one Saturday afternoon, about a month before her death, when I'd visited her at the hospital. On her bedside TV set she'd tuned in a panel discussion among young Peace Corps workers. I sat quietly beside her bed until the program was over.

She turned to me then, a warm smile on her thin face. "Cathy, maybe it's because I have you, or maybe it's just because I'm an optimistic fool. But do you know who I trust to keep this planet from blowing itself up? You under-thirties. Oh, life's going to be pretty unsettling for quite a while after your generation takes over, but I think a better world's going to come out of it all—kinder, and more fulfilling, and more—joyous."

Now Loren Hauklid was saying, "And those so-called hunters who come out here from New York each fall! They buy a red cap, and an expensive gun, and blaze away at anything that moves. Several times damn fools have thought our Leghorns were pheasants. So now, during the hunting season, I keep driving through these woods with the Dobermans. Word gets around that it would be smart to respect those no-trespassing signs."

He stopped speaking. After a moment my aunt said, "Catherine, you must be tired. I'll bet you'd like to go to bed." Then, as if afraid I'd think she was trying to shunt me off upstairs, she gave me a nervous smile and added, "Although I suppose you'd like to watch the ten o'clock news first."

"Yes, I'd like to."

We returned through the warm darkness to the house. When we entered the living room, Byron was still hunched before the TV set. On the screen a villainous-faced man in western clothes stood drinking at an ornate bar. Suddenly he caught sight in the long mirror of a white-hatted man—probably the same one who'd been on the horse—entering the barroom. The first man whirled, firing from the hip. The camera, still trained on the mirrored reflection of the newcomer, showed him returning the fire. The villainous-faced man crumpled to the floor.

I gave a low, relieved laugh. When the Hauklids looked at me questioningly, I said, pitching my voice below the sounds coming from the TV set, "That explains something that happened before you came home this afternoon. You know that big tilting mirror in my room? Well, Byron saw me looking into it. He said something about the one in the mirror shooting the other one. For a moment or two I was—upset. I mean, he was so insistent that one would almost have thought— But now I realize he was describing something he'd seen on TV many times. I mean, that barroom-mirror bit is a standard scene in Westerns."

Loren Hauklid was looking at his son's brown head and hunched shoulders. "Yes, they use that scene a lot."

I glanced at my aunt. She too stared at Byron. And her face was so green-white that alarm shot through me. I cried, "What is it? Are you ill?"

She jerked her face around toward me. "It's nothing." Her pale lips stretched into a smile. "Just a little palpitation. I have it sometimes after meals. Let's sit down. That program will be over soon, and then we can watch the news."

An hour later, after I'd watched the news, after I'd taken a long, and I hoped relaxing, bath in the wood-enclosed tub, I slipped quietly into the room where my daughter slept. But when I'd stretched out in the double bed, I found that, tired as I was, I couldn't sleep. I lay rigid there in the dark, listening to Nicole's quiet breathing over there in the railed bed, and watching the faces that drifted before my mind's eye. Loren Hauklid's handsome one, suffused with bitter scorn there in his workshed. My aunt's, so worn and tense that, if it hadn't been for old snapshots of her my mother had shown me, I wouldn't have been able to visualize the smiling, gentle-faced twenty-year-old Loren had fallen in love with. Byron's face, so innocent and open and eager for approval. And my mother's, as it had looked three nights before her death, so thin there in the glow of the green-shaded bedside light, and yet so alive with the changing expressions her memories sent across it—tenderness, and sorrow, and regret.

A summer storm had been beating at the hospital windows that night. Often I'd had to lean close to distinguish her words. "Catherine," she'd begun, "I want to talk to you." After a pause she went on, "You know I loved your father, don't you?"

I said wonderingly, "Of course I know it." I could remember from my Philadelphia childhood how happy her face had looked whenever the three of us had been out together. Oh, we never did anything especially festive—trips to the zoo, a tour of Constitution Hall, things like that—but I could remember how delighted I felt to be out with the two of them, and how happy they'd seemed in each other's company, and in mine. Too, I could remember the terrified rebellion I'd glimpsed for a moment in my mother's face the day my father was called to serve in the Korean War. And I could remember her face, grief-ravaged and yet proud, on that day nearly a year later, when she and I stood in Arlington Cemetery, and uniformed men fired a farewell volley over my father's grave.

"I want to be sure you know I loved him deeply." A gust of rain struck the hospital window like flung gravel, and I leaned closer to hear her words. "Because I want to tell you about someone else—earlier. I have to tell you, Cathy. Someday you and Nicole may need to go to your grandfather's house. And if so, it's better that you go there knowing—all the facts."

Sitting there beside her bed, I'd felt my body turn cold. I knew at that moment that she didn't expect to survive her coming operation. I said, in a voice that sounded high-pitched and childish even to my own ears, "Mother? Mother?"

"Sh-h-h! Let me talk, dear. I don't feel awfully well, and it's going to be hard to talk of these things to my own daughter, so don't make it harder for me."

She drew a deep breath. "Now you've always known that there was—trouble. You've known that I was disinherited, and that I went to New York. Later the New York store I worked for sent me to its Philadelphia branch, and I met your father there. You've known all that."

Dumbly, I nodded. I'd known even more. In some way

—I couldn't say just how—I'd gained the impression that the events of that summer four years before my own birth had involved some entanglement between my mother and her sister's husband.

She said, "There was this young man, Loren Hauklid. Your grandfather hired him to manage the Jessup place. Loren had never ever been on eastern Long Island before, but from the start he fitted in. It wasn't just us girls who liked him. He was popular with all the young people. I remember the wonderful cookouts we used to have on the front lawn after Loren came to live with us. Older people liked him, too. When he'd been there less than a year, he was invited to join the Neptague Volunteer Firemen. You wouldn't know about that, Cathy, but in small towns that's a great honor.

"As for Loren and your grandfather—well, Loren's parents were both dead, back in the Minnesota town where he'd been born. And your grandfather had always wanted a son. It was natural that they'd grow very close. When Marian and Loren fell in love and decided to marry, your grandfather was so pleased that he gave them a wedding trip to Norway, to see the village where Loren's parents had been born."

The low, breathy voice went on to say that in those days, the late nineteen-thirties, most people still crossed the Atlantic by boat. She and my grandfather had accompanied the newlyweds to a Hudson River pier in New York. "I was terribly excited by the romance of it, and I thought Loren was handsome and wonderful. Any seventeen-year-old would have. I hoped that someday I'd find a man like that who'd fall in love with me. But that's all I felt, then."

That fall, shortly after the Hauklids returned from Norway, my mother had gone away to a two-year college for women in New Hampshire. When she came home for the Christmas holidays, she found everything going wonderfully well—Loren and my grandfather deep in plans for next year's planting, and all three of them looking forward to the birth of Marian's child in late spring.

"Byron was a beautiful baby, Catherine. It never occurred to any of us that there could be anything wrong with him."

In fact, it wasn't until more than a year later that the Hauklids began to worry. Until then they'd kept telling themselves that many babies are a little "slow." But when he'd entered his sixteenth month and still hadn't spoken, or even tried to walk, their local pediatrician recommended that they consult a New York specialist.

"I'd realized it must be awful for them, but until I came home after finishing my two-year course, I didn't know just how awful. Their tragedy, instead of drawing them together, was driving them apart. Much as I sympathized with Marian, I felt that their growing estrangement was largely her fault. In her suffering, she'd begun to lash out at Loren. One Sunday at dinner, for instance, she told us that she'd been looking back through all the family records she could find. There'd never been any sort of retardation or other mental trouble, she said, in the Jessup family. I looked at Loren, and saw so much pain in his eyes that I wondered how he could stand it."

Late that summer, Marian had taken Byron to a clinic in upstate New York for a two weeks' series of tests. "She'd been gone only a day or two when I walked back through the woods to Aunt Amy's house. I've told you about Amy Jessup, the old, old spinster, the one who made the staircase runner with the seals of the thirteen original states. Well, I guess she'd always been a little eccentric, in spite of what Marian said about there being nothing of that sort in our family. Anyway, a year or so after the Civil War, when she was still a young woman, she'd persuaded the family to build her an octagonal summerhouse more than a mile from the main house. As children, Marian and I used to play there.

"Well, I went there that afternoon. When I walked in, I saw Loren standing in the middle of the floor, his back to me. He was crying—great sobs that sounded as if they were going to tear his lungs apart. It's a terrible thing to hear a man cry. And it was especially terrible to hear a man of only twenty-five crying as if he had no hope left, no hope at all.

"He heard me, and wheeled around. We looked at each other. I don't know which of us took the first step. I just know that we were in each other's arms, both crying. And then after a while, we weren't crying—"

That was the start of it. For more than a week, they met each day in the summerhouse. "Perhaps it had begun out of loneliness and pain on his part, and pity and admiration on mine. But soon it was something more, at least for me. Oh, I was aware all the time that it was wrong, according to every tenet by which I'd been raised. I also knew that even if we weren't discovered, I'd suffer in the months ahead, because Loren would remain my sister's husband. I couldn't have brought myself to take him away from her, even if he'd been willing to leave her. But at the time, none of that seemed to matter, or at least not enough."

The day before Marian's return, an itinerant worker on the place, hired for the field corn harvest, saw them leaving the summerhouse. He told my grandfather.

My grandfather's wrath was of Old Testament proportions. When Marian returned, he called the three young people together. His whorish younger daughter—"Yes," my mother said, "he actually used that phrase"—was no longer welcome under his roof. He would give her a thousand dollars. No doubt when that was gone she'd know how to obtain more. Aside from the thousand, she'd get nothing from him, either now or after his death. And then he told them the terms of his new will.

"I went to New York that night," my mother said, "and a few days later found a job in a department store. As soon as I could, I sent my father a certified check for the thousand dollars. He kept the check, but didn't answer the letter I'd sent with it. And four months after I left home, he died. I've so often wished that he'd lived a few more years, long enough to know that I'd made a success of my job, and married a fine man, and had you. Oh, not that it would have made him change his will. He was too stubborn for that. But at least he'd have had a better opinion of me."

After a moment I said, "And you never went back to my grandfather's house, except for his funeral." It was a statement, not a question. I knew that within my own memory she hadn't gone back.

"No, and even for the funeral I didn't stay overnight. I took the first train back to New York. After I married your father, I wrote Marian that we'd both like to come for a visit. Her reply wasn't—hostile. But it wasn't favorable, either. She said that she felt that under the circumstances, our visit wouldn't be a happy one. She didn't say what circumstances. Perhaps she meant that she still felt—bitter toward me, although her letter didn't sound bitter. I tried again after you were born. Her answer was much the same. Since then I've waited for her to invite me. She hasn't."

"Did—did Loren Hauklid ever write to you?"

"Once, soon after I left your grandfather's house for New York. He must have seen my return address on the envelope in which I'd sent the thousand-dollar check. It was a beautiful letter, and so—so honest. But obviously he neither expected nor wanted me to answer it."

She paused, and for a moment I thought she was going

to tell me what was in the letter. Instead she said, "I hope Marian and Loren have managed to have a reasonably happy life together. Perhaps, if they'd had other children — But maybe Marian was afraid to take the chance."

She fell silent, and closed her eyes. After a moment she opened them, and smiled at me. "I'm a little tired now, dear. Perhaps I'd better sleep."

I rang for the nurse, bent and kissed her cool, dry forehead, and left her. Four days later she was dead.

Now, there in the darkened bedroom of my grandfather's house, I felt I couldn't lie still any longer. Getting up, I moved quietly past Nicole's bed to stand at the window. The pale green glow of fireflies still drifted through the trees on the opposite side of the farmyard. Above the trees, stars were bright in a no longer hazy sky, giving promise that tomorrow would be less humid.

Probably, I reflected, the Loren Hauklid I'd met today had changed little physically since my mother knew him. He was still handsome, still lean and tall. But otherwise, I felt, she would scarcely have recognized that bitter-voiced man in the workshed as the one she'd fallen in love with so disastrously. Did the years often change people that much? I hoped not.

Or could it be that he hadn't changed? Maybe he'd always been like that. Perhaps it was just that she in her pity and her young infatuation—after all, she'd been barely out of her teens—had seen in him only what she wanted to see.

Perhaps, I reflected, no one ever really knows anyone else.

One thing was certain. My mother's hope that the Hauklids had achieved a reasonable degree of happiness together hadn't been fulfilled. The very air of this old house seemed heavy with unhappiness, and with some deep, longstanding anxiety.

As I stood there, it seemed to me I could sense

something else in this house. A frightened hatred, swirling up staircases and along hallways, seeping under the door of this room like an invisible fog—

I gave myself a mental shake. Overtiredness was affecting my good sense. You could perhaps sense hatred if you were in the hater's presence, but otherwise not. Besides, who in this house could have reason to either hate or fear my little girl and me? Both the Hauklids might feel exasperation over our intrusion into their isolated household, but surely they didn't hate me.

Just the same, I said a silent prayer that I'd find a job the next day. I'd save money as fast as I could, so that I could take Nicole and myself away from this house.

I started to turn back toward my bed and then paused, arrested by something I'd glimpsed deep among the trees, far over to my right. A gleam of light. It winked out, and then almost immediately came on again. A flashlight? A lantern blocked momentarily from my view as it was carried behind a tree trunk?

Remembering what Loren had said in his workshed, I thought, "Poachers." I had a vague impression that some animals—muskrats, for instance—were hunted at night. The intruder or intruders apparently were quite some distance away—either that, or upwind from the kennel. Otherwise the Dobermans would have been making an uproar.

A whimsical thought struck me. Perhaps the dogs didn't bark because it was their owner out there, searching in the dead of night for the family jewels, buried long ago by my grandfather. The idea amused me by its very unlikelihood. In the first place, I knew that the unfrivolous New England Jessups had never gone in for jewelry. Even my mother, true to her upbringing, had never owned any jewelry except a cultured pearl necklace my father had given her. In the second place, it was impossible to connect my grandfather with so fanciful an act as burying valuables. Plainly he'd been a no-nonsense sort of person, with an abiding faith in the Scriptures and four-percent bonds. No, it was trespassers out there.

Trespassers. The man in the Jessup graveyard that afternoon. But surely it wasn't he out there with that flashlight or lantern. There'd been nothing about him to suggest a poacher.

Would I see him again? Very probably, if I stayed more than a few days in a community this small. I wondered if he were married. Perhaps so, but there'd been sort of an unsettled look about him that made me think he wasn't.

No, it had been more than an unsettled look. It seemed to me now that as we stared at each other across the little cemetery, his face had been both wary and purposeful, like that of an Indian brave who'd slipped into an enemy tribe's territory—

An Indian brave! If a history professor with an interest in old graveyards could remind me of Uncas, then I must be overtired indeed. Still, I found it pleasant as well as disturbing that my thoughts, for the first time since Bill's death, were lingering over another man.

Turning, I walked back to my bed.

5

The orange-red light of a newly risen sun, striking through the bedroom window into my eyes, awoke me the next morning. From somewhere behind the house came the unfamiliar but pleasantly bucolic sound of crowing roosters. Slipping out of bed, I crossed in my bare feet to stand at the window.

Fat pink clouds floated in the blue morning sky. Among the trees across the clearing, standing motionless in full summer dress, a dawn mist still hovered, stained a faint, opalescent pink by the sunrise light. The effect was magically lovely. Even the bare yard, stained that same faint pink, and with drops of dew glinting like diamonds in the few tufts of coarse grass, didn't look ugly today.

Nor did I feel depressed and apprehensive. In fact, as I leaned my palms on the window sill, and drew cool morning air deep into my lungs, I felt my spirits rising, right along with the sun. We'd made it, Nicole and I. No matter how shabby this house to which we'd come, or how troubled its older occupants, we'd be assured of food and shelter here. And I'd find a job today. Somehow I was sure of it.

What's more, this isolated house was still part of the Hamptons, that fabulous area I'd read about, and heard about from my mother. Beyond these woods were lovely villages that dated from Colonial times, and beaches, and summer theaters, and restaurants where the beautiful and famous displayed their deep tans and fashionable clothes—

I thought, "Why, I'm actually looking forward to staying here!" Remembering my gloom of the night before, I gave a low laugh. Then, swiftly, I turned to look down at Nicole. No, I hadn't disturbed her. She lay asleep, one hand loosely curled on the pillow like a pink and white flower, and looking so angelic that one would have thought she never had a temper tantrum, or refused to eat her vegetables, or failed to put her toys away.

Tiptoeing to the stand beside my bed, I lifted my watch. A little after six. Since Loren had no job to go to, probably none of the Hauklids would be up at this hour. But surely they wouldn't mind my making breakfast for myself. I slipped my watch onto my wrist, put on my blue quilted robe and matching slippers, and crossed to the bathroom. A few minutes later, with the taste of tooth powder still pleasant in my mouth, I descended the stairs and walked back along the stretch of ugly brown linoleum to the kitchen.

My aunt, in a clean but faded cotton print dress, sat at the enamel-topped kitchen table, a coffee cup and a half-eaten piece of toast before her. I said, "Oh, good morning. I didn't think anyone would be up yet."

She got to her feet. "I'm always up early. I don't need much sleep." From the look of her, she'd had almost none the night before. "What would you like for breakfast?"

"Oh, please. Don't wait on me."

"Let me wait on you, at least this first morning. You've been ill, remember."

Plainly she was trying to make me feel a little less unwelcome. "All right. Thanks." I sat down in the chair opposite hers. "But this morning I don't feel as if I've been ill." I didn't. Maybe the clean Long Island air and at least temporary respite from financial anxiety were already restoring my strength.

"Just the same, you must be careful. Now there's grapefruit juice, if you don't mind it canned. And cornflakes, and eggs, of course."

"Juice and cornflakes and coffee sound wonderful."

As she walked over to the refrigerator, she asked, "How'd you sleep?"

"Fine, once I got to sleep." I paused and then said, "I saw a light somewhere over in the woods last night."

She'd opened the refrigerator door and bent slightly to look in. For several seconds she remained in that attitude, as if unable to locate the fruit juice. Then she reached in, took out a tall can, closed the refrigerator door, and walked over to the sink. "Where?" she asked.

Remembering where the sun had risen, I said, "Southeast of the house. I couldn't judge how far away the light was."

"Poachers, hunting in Jethro's Hole."

"In what?"

"Swamps used to be called holes. The one about a mile southeast of this house was named after Jethro Jessup. He was your great-great—oh, I don't know how many greats. Anyway, he was the first Jessup to own this land."

She poured grapefruit juice into a glass and then added, "Please don't mention the light to Loren. Trespassers—upset him."

"I won't." Should I tell her about that other trespasser? Perhaps I should, especially considering where I'd found him. "There was a trespasser in the woods yesterday afternoon, too, but I'm sure he was no poacher."

Back turned, she'd reached up to open the door of the

dish cupboard. Now she again stood motionless, fingers curled around the handle. "Where was he?"

I described the incident in the little graveyard. "It was a bit nervy of him, considering all those no-trespassing signs. But I'm sure he's all right. I suppose it's natural that a history professor should be interested in old graveyards."

She'd finished placing my breakfast on a tray. Now she carried it over to the table. "Lots of people like to read inscriptions on old tombstones. What did you say his name was? Philip Owen?"

"That's right."

She sat down opposite me. "You didn't say what he looked like."

Remembering my fancy of the night before, I said, "Rather like a gray-eyed Indian. Think, dark-haired, heavily tanned, early thirties—"

"Well, please don't tell Loren about that, either. Like you, I'm sure the man was all right. But Loren just can't stand any kind of intruders."

"I won't say anything."

We stopped speaking. After a moment another thought struck me. I asked, "What happened to the little finger on his left hand?"

"He broke it in a fall from a horse when he was a child, and it wasn't set properly." As soon as she'd spoken, an appalled look came into her eyes, and her face lost color. Puzzled and embarrassed, I averted my gaze.

A few moments later she asked, "Are you going to look for a job today?"

I looked back at her. "Yes. Any suggestions?"

"The *Neptague Messenger,* our weekly paper, carries want ads. Maybe the edition that came out last Thursday has been sold out at the stationery store. But the newspaper office itself probably still has copies."

"I'll go there."

We sipped coffee in silence. Then she said, in a strained tone, "One thing I forgot to ask. Did you notice the hook on your bedroom door?"

"Yes." I'd also noticed that it looked brand-new.

"I lost the key to that door long ago, so I put the hook on yesterday. Not that there's any danger," she added hastily. "It's just that Byron—well, he walks in his sleep sometimes, the way many—"

She broke off, but I knew she'd been about to say, "the way many children do." After a moment she went on, "I've never known him to wander over to the north wing, but he might. I wouldn't want you to be—startled, so you'd better hook your door at night."

"I will." And I most certainly would. Reason tells me that a sleepwalker is the most helpless and harmless of creatures. And yet to me the very idea of sleepwalking is uncomfortably eerie.

She changed the subject. "Nicole looks like you, and the way your mother did when she was a tiny girl. All except the brown eyes. I guess she got those from her father."

"Yes, Bill's eyes were brown."

While I finished my breakfast, we chatted about Nicole. Together we washed and dried the dishes we'd used. Then I glanced at my watch. Still only a few minutes past seven, far too early for job-hunting.

I said, "I'd love to go for a walk. But I suppose I'd better wake Nicole and give her breakfast."

"Don't wake her. Just take your walk. She needs that sleep. Traveling's hard on young children."

"But if she wakes up—"

"Until Loren and Byron want breakfast, I'll be rearranging the upstairs linen closet. It's only a few feet from the second-floor landing. I'll be sure to hear her if she wakes up."

I said gratefully, "Thanks a lot. I would like that walk, but I want her to have her sleep, too."

Going upstairs, I dressed quickly and quietly in an old skirt, sleeveless white cotton blouse, and tennis sneakers. When I emerged from the room, leaving the door open, I saw my aunt. A pile of sheets cradled in one arm, she stood at the open door of a closet just beyond the landing, in the original part of the house. She gave her nervous smile, and laid one finger to her lips. Returning her smile, I went quietly down the stairs, out the front door, and across the barren yard to the woods.

Always, ever since I was a little girl vacationing with my parents in eastern Pennsylvania, I've loved the early morning woods. As I moved along the narrow road, I thought of a pre-sunrise walk I'd taken with my father through some woods in Bucks County. I was seven then. To my wonder and delight, the birds at that early hour hadn't been fully awake yet. One towhee, perched on a lower branch of a young oak, had allowed me to walk right up to him. Ruffling his feathers and chirping drowsily, he stared back at me with sherry-brown eyes still glazed with sleep.

Now, of course, around an hour past sunrise, the birds were fully awake, rustling food for themselves, and in some cases, I suppose, for a second brood of nestlings. Bluejays teetered on pitch pine boughs and jeered at me. A cardinal, scarlet as blood except for the heavy dark line on his cheek and throat, flashed across the road. In the bare and lifeless top branches of a tall old oak, several crows carried on what sounded like a blasphemous quarrel.

Here was a little footpath, branching off to the left. I turned onto it, drawing the acrid tang of oak leaves and the resinous one of pine deep into my lungs, and delighting in the way the still-low sun sent slanted beams of light through breaks in woodland. In the spring, probably, pink lady's-slippers bloomed in these woods. No lady's-slippers now, of course, but I did see woodland gerardia, each plant shaped like a tiny apple tree, with widely spread branches bearing rose-purple flowers rather than fruit. And in one open spot the ground was golden with broad-leaved asters.

Still another branching path. After a moment's hesitation, I took it. Even if I become so lost that I couldn't retrace my steps, my sense of direction was good enough that I'd be able to find my way back to the private road.

I moved on, to a steadily swelling chorus of bird voices. I had a companion now. A catbird, her lines racy as a sailing yacht's, flew a few feet inside the first line of trees, sometimes a yard or so ahead of me, sometimes behind, but always regarding me with a bright, inquisitive eye as she passed me.

Turning a bend in the tunnel-like path, I saw brightness ahead. A clearing, already bathed in sunlight. I hurried toward it and then, at the end of the path, stopped short.

A summerhouse. An octagonal summerhouse, its sides made of wood from the stone foundation to about four feet above the ground. From that point to the overhanging eaves, the sides were screened. Beyond the screening hung what looked like wide bamboo blinds.

For a moment more I stood motionless, and then, irresistibly drawn, moved slowly across the clearing toward the closed door of the summerhouse. As I walked, I had an odd feeling that the year was 1940, and that I was a twenty-year-old named Caroline Jessup—

But when at the top of the three low steps I'd grasped the knob and swung the unlocked door back, I saw no tall man, no young husband and father, sobbing out his sorrow. I saw no one at all.

But the summerhouse was still in use. Enough light came through the loosely woven blinds to show me that. On a wicker table against one wall of the eight-sided room stood an oil lamp and a transistor radio. On the shelf below was a tray holding a half-empty bourbon bottle and two thick glasses that once must have held jelly. In the center of the room, two wicker armchairs had been drawn up to a card table. And against another section of wall stood a daybed, covered with a spread of yellow-flowered cotton. Beside it, a flimsy-looking nightstand of brown veneer held a large black plastic ashtray.

Moving across the room, I looked down at the tray. It held stubs of several filter-tip cigarettes, each stained with orange lipstick. Not my aunt's, surely. I hadn't seen her smoke. Besides, it was usually redheads who wore that shade of lipstick.

A paperback book lay on the stand's shelf. Bending, I picked it up. It was entitled *The Serving Wench.* On the cover a woman, naked to the waist, stood in the embrace of a leering man in a stovepipe hat and a frock coat. Above the picture were the words: "Read it now! The long-suppressed classic about the sort of Victorians Queen Victoria never met." The publisher had been a firm which specializes in bringing out such "long-suppressed classics."

Someone had used a bobbie pin as a bookmark. I opened the book to those pages. In one margin was a stain, probably made by a fingertip, of the same orange lipstick that was on the cigarette ends.

Restoring the book to its place, I stood looking around the room. On the card table were two balls of crumpled yellow paper. Moving to the table, I smoothed out one crumpled sheet, and then the other.

The first bore a rough sketch of a football player, standing on tiptoe in his heavy shoes, and clasping a ball in his two upraised hands. In the second sketch, the player's right arm had been brought up and back, ready to throw a pass.

"I designed this one last week," Loren Hauklid had said, picking up the little ceramic football player, "and turned the first batch out yesterday."

So one day or evening last week he'd sat here at this table, and drawn his sketches, and made his choice between them. Perhaps his woman companion had sat in the second armchair, making comments and suggestions. Or perhaps she'd lain over there on the daybed, reading her paperback.

His woman companion. Red-haired, probably, with perhaps a taste for bourbon, and almost certainly a taste for gamy literature. And he met her here, where once he and young Caroline Jessup had stood weeping in each other's arms—

I felt thankful that my mother would never know about that.

Did Aunt Marian know? And if so, did she care? Well, it was none of my business, I told myself, trying to hold onto the hopeful, even happy mood I'd enjoyed as I moved along the woodland path. My business was to find a job, and save money, and take Nicole back to Chicago.

I glanced at my watch. Almost eight. By the time I reached Neptague, stores and offices would be open. Quickly, wishing I'd managed to fight off the compulsion that had drawn me in there, I left the summerhouse and closed the door behind me.

Now I saw that, on opposite sides of the clearing, two roads that were little more than car tracks led away through the trees. Realizing it would probably bring me to the Hauklids' private road, I hurried toward the set of tracks on my left.

6

As I emerged from the road into the farmyard about ten minutes later, movement at a second-floor window of the south wing caught my eye. A curtain, released by a man's hand, fell back into place. Byron's hand? No, if it were Byron up there, he'd have called out to me. That must be Loren's room.

Probably all the Hauklids slept in the south wing. Even so, there must be several empty rooms in that part of the house in which they could have placed Nicole and me. (My great-grandfather, who added those wings, had not only been the most prosperous of the Jessups, with income from whaling as well as farming, but he'd also been the most prolific, siring two sons and seven daughters. Hence all those additional rooms for family members and servants.) But instead of assigning us to a room near themselves, the Hauklids had put us away off in the north wing. Not that I wasn't just as glad. But it was still another bit of evidence, as if I needed more, that my aunt and uncle had contemplated our impending arrival with something less than jubilation.

Soundless in my tennis sneakers, I crossed the little porch and started to open the screen door.

"Yes, Philip Owen," I heard my aunt say. Her voice was low, hurried. And by the direction from which it came, I knew she must be speaking into the phone, there on its table near the foot of the stairs. "Oh, no!" she went on. "Don't ring his office. It's just that we once knew him slightly, and we heard he was on the faculty. If he is, we'll get in touch with him later. . . . Oh, he is,"

She'd said it was Loren who became "upset" over trespassing. And yet she herself was checking up on the man I'd met in the little graveyard. Knowing that she'd be embarrassed if I walked in now, I moved to one side of the little porch and stood looking out over the yard.

I could still hear her. "But I'm wondering if it's the same Philip Owen." She gave her nervous laugh. "After all, it's a common name. The one we knew—oh, he'd be in his early thirties now. Thin and dark, and with gray eyes, if I remember rightly.— Yes, I guess it must be the same man.—No, no message. Good-by, and thank you." I heard her footsteps going toward the rear of the house.

For at least another minute I stood gazing out over the yard. Could Loren look down and see my odd behavior? A glance at the window where I'd seen the curtain moved assured me he couldn't, not unless he unlatched the screen and leaned out.

Surely I'd stayed here long enough. Opening the screen door, I let it close behind me with a distinct bang. As I walked back toward the kitchen, I heard Nicole's voice, sounding excited and happy. I found her and Byron seated at the enamel-topped table, both spooning oatmeal. Propped on a chair between them was the Raggedy Ann doll.

Turning away from the sink, my aunt gave me her tense little smile. "I found some oatmeal I'd forgot I had. I hope it was the right thing to—"

"Of course it was."

Byron said, "You going to eat breakfast with us, Catherine?"

"I've had breakfast." At his disappointed expression, I added, "I mustn't eat two breakfasts, Byron. They'd make me fat."

I looked at my daughter, expecting to see an accusatory, you-sneaked-off-without-me look in her eyes. But the smile she gave me, slightly marred by a dab of oatmeal on her lower lip, was radiant.

"Enjoying your breakfast?" I asked.

"Yes! And after breakfast Aunt Marian and Byron and I are going to gather eggs! And we're going out to the tool shed. There's a cat with *kittens* in the tool shed."

Thank heavens, I thought, that she gave promise of growing up less thin-skinned than her Mama. Something as intangible as an atmosphere didn't bother her, not for long. With a new doll beside her, and the prospect of egg-gathering and kitten-stroking ahead of her, she'd forgotten her dismay at first sight of "our new home."

I smiled gratefully at my aunt. "I hope she won't be too much trouble. Here you haven't even finished serving breakfasts yet. I mean, Loren isn't down, is he?"

Somehow, perhaps because I knew of his long-ago involvement with my mother, I couldn't call him Uncle Loren. If my aunt noticed the omission, she gave no sign. "Loren's never much of an early bird."

"But he's awake," Byron said. "I heard him moving around." He turned to me. "Papa's room is next to mine."

Not Papa and Mama's room. Well, no business of mine, nor did I want it to be.

"I'd better get upstairs now," I said, "and bring down my job-hunting dress. It needs pressing."

Less than an hour later, I parked my car at one end of Neptague's wide main street. I was careful not to rumple my brown linen dress, the best summer outfit I owned, as

I got out. It was of two pieces—a pleated skirt and an overblouse, white-belted and sleeveless. Because I'd lost weight, its skirt hung longer on me than when I'd bought it the summer before. But that, I felt, was all to the good, since it probably made me look more dignified and businesslike.

Finding the newspaper office was no problem. Midway of the first block of Neptague's three-block business district, sandwiched in between a dress shop and a bank, was a one-story structure of red brick. Its plate-glass window bore the words *"Neptague Messenger. Steve Connery, Ed. and Pub."*

As I stepped inside, I heard a rhythmic slamming sound from behind the beaverboard partition that formed the rear wall of the little office. On this side of the partition, a man sat with his feet up on a cluttered desk, a magazine and a pencil in his hands. When he saw me, he took his feet down and laid the magazine and pencil on the desk.

I glanced at the open pages. The right-hand one bore a Double-Crostic, with about half the spaces penciled in. He must have noticed my looking at the puzzle, because he grinned and said, "The office usually isn't like this. Most days it's a madhouse. Reporters racing in and out. Somebody yelling for the copyboy every thirty seconds. And me shouting into the pressroom phone, 'Stand by to replate!' "

"I can imagine."

"But Wednesdays are slow because the paper goes to press on Wednesday. That's the banging noise you hear."

"It doesn't sound the way it does in those old movies on TV. Their presses rumble."

"Bogart movies. The front pages keep streaming out, with the headline, 'Heiress Elopes with Gang Leader.' Those are roller presses. Ours is a flatbed press. Now what can I do for you? I'm Steve Connery, by the way, Ed. and Pub., and at your service."

"Do you have a copy of last week's newspaper?"

"Maybe. Usually we have plenty left over. But last week we sold out. The paper carried the story of the Volunteer Firemans' Festival. Just about everyone in town was in on that, and they all wanted to read their names in the paper. But we still may have a copy around."

Getting up, he moved toward the opening in the partition. I guessed he was about thirty-seven, a tall man with straight brown hair receding at the temples. His face was bony—prominent brow ridges and cheekbones, aquiline nose, wide mouth, square chin. It was the kind of face that might belong to a religious ascetic, or the most hardened cynic. In fact, to judge by portraits I'd seen in museums, both Savonarola and Machiavelli had that sort of face.

He yelled, "Jim!" The clatter ceased. "We got a copy of last week's paper back there?"

"I guess so."

A few moments later a youth of about nineteen, wearing a brown beanie with its cuffed edge cut in a sawtooth design, poked a grease-stained face around the partition. His outstretched hand, also grease-stained, held a thin newspaper. His boss took it, and the youth disappeared. The slamming noise resumed.

Taking the paper from Steve Connery, I asked, "How much is it?"

"Ten cents, but that one's not for sale. It may be the only one I have for the files. But you can sit down over there by the window and look up whatever you want."

"Thank you."

Going to a wooden armchair beside the plate-glass window, I sat down and opened the paper. The classifieds were on page three. The Neptague Lumber Company wanted a general office worker. Someone needed a practical nurse to care for an elderly woman, no cooking or housework. The Montauk Drive-in Theater wanted a box office girl. I'd try the lumber company first, I decided, and then the theater.

I said, "Could you tell me where the lumber company and the drive-in theater are?"

"Yes, but it would do you no good." He was leaning against the side of the desk now, arms folded and ankles crossed. "Both those jobs are gone. The practical nurse job isn't. The woman's daughter has put the ad in again this week. But I wouldn't apply, if I were you. That old lady threw hot tea on her last nurse.

"Your best bet," he went on, "would be the fancy restaurants around here. They hire their waitresses—college girls, mainly—at the beginning of the season, but there might still be some openings. The pay's not bad, and the tips are very good."

I felt the first twinges of alarm. Perhaps jobs here weren't as plentiful as I'd assumed. "The trouble is that I'm not supposed to take a strenuous job. I had pneumonia not too long ago."

"Tough. Well, go next door to the bank. They need an office girl. Their ad's in the edition we're printing right now. You'll get a head start on all my other readers."

I said, rising, "Thank you very much."

"Wait a minute. You got a place to stay? I know of two girls you could move in with."

"Thank you, but I'm staying with Mr. and Mrs. Hauklid. I'm their niece."

Two or three seconds passed before he asked, "Loren Hauklid's niece?"

Odd, I thought. Philip Owen had asked that same question.

"Mrs. Hauklid's. Well, good-by, and thanks again." I started toward the door.

"Hold on. How'd you like to work here?"

"Here?" I looked around the little office. "But do you need anyone?"

"Sure. This summer I've had two different assistants, both male. Neither of them worked out. Maybe a girl would. Anyway, I need someone to hold down the office while I'm out hustling ads. That's where the money is in country journalism—ads and job printing. The ten cents a copy my readers pay doesn't even cover the cost of the paper it's printed on."

He paused, and then added, "I'll pay eighty a week, the same as the bank, and I flatter myself this will be a lot more interesting job. Sure, I know almost any office job in New York would pay more than that, but then, think what living in New York or any big city costs."

Eighty a week, I thought, my spirits rising, and I'd be able to save almost all of it. "But do you think that someone with no newspaper experience—"

"I'm not looking for a Nellie Bly. Your main responsibility will be the 'Our Neighbors' column. You'll call up people—local people, not summer people—and ask if they have any social news. Then you'll write things like: 'Mr. and Mrs. John Malone were hosts to their daughter and son-in-law, Mr. and Mrs. James Doyle of Brooklyn, over the weekend.' Or, 'The Thomas Blakes' twin daughters celebrated their tenth birthday with a lawn party last Tuesday. Happy birthday, Jane and Janet!' Get all the names you can in every issue, and get all the names right. Nothing seems to make people madder than having their names misspelled. Think you can do that?"

"I don't see why not."

"What's your name?"

"Catherine Morrel."

"How much do you know about the Hampton's, Cathy?"

"Almost nothing, except what I've read. I got here just yesterday."

He opened the door. "Come on, then."

"Where are we going?"

"Orientation tour." Hand still on the doorknob, he yelled, "Jim!"

The noisy press fell silent. After a moment the grease-stained young man appeared in the partition doorway. "Hold the fort. If anybody comes in with a display ad or some job printing, get the money in advance."

Out in the street, he opened the door of a dark blue convertible. "We'll go to Southampton first, and see how the other one-tenth of one percent lives."

We did, driving out Montauk Highway past level potato fields and through tree-shaded villages, to the oddly named but awesomely elegant Gin Lane section of Southampton. On the curving sidewalks imported English nursemaids, with streamers fluttering from their caps, wheeled imported English prams. Set back on sweeping lawns, or rising from behind high walls, were Tudor manor houses, Italian villas, Colonial mansions. In four blocks I counted as many chauffeur-driven Rolls-Royces. My employer, chatty as a tour guide, reeled off famous names—the Winston Guests, the Henry Fords, the Windsors—as he pointed out various houses. Then, taking another road, we looped back toward Negtague and the villages beyond.

He talked almost constantly, drawing for me a sort of social profile of the Hamptons. First, he said, there were the local people—farmers, shopkeepers, fishermen, skilled workmen, and professional people. Then there were the summer people, some of them only modestly affluent, but many of them indisputably rich.

The jet set rich, he said, tended to prefer Southampton. The more conservative rich summered in East Hampton.

"People bring their chauffeurs with them to Southampton. In East Hampton that's considered rather bad form."

And then, he said, there were the artists and writers. Most of them summered in East Hampton or Springs, although a few chose Sag Harbor.

"Then there are the groupers, New York young people, men and women, who pool their money to rent a big house, and then sleep as many as a half-dozen to a room. Lots of brouhaha about the groupers. And lately there've been bands of well-heeled hippies coming out here and making the nights throb with their electric guitars. Even more brouhaha about the hippies."

As I listened to him and watched the other cars streaming along an asphalt road between walls of oak and pitch pine—family groups in station wagons, two young women of almost cover-girl loveliness in a white Triumph, a bearded man, shoulder-length brown hair held back by a beaded headband, in a blood-red Ferrari—I thought of the Hauklids, shut away deep in the woods from all this color and excitement. Now and then I saw narrow dirt roads branching off the highway. Did some of them lead to other such households, people almost as cut off from the present-day Hamptons as if they'd died thirty or forty years ago? I thought of my aunt saying, "Why, the very best motels out here used to charge only six dollars a day."

Beside me, my companion made an exclamation. "Man! Am I the eagle-eyed journalist. I didn't notice your wedding ring until just now." He paused. "Separated from your husband?"

"No. He was—killed last winter."

"Vietnam?"

"A car accident."

"I'm sorry."

A few minutes later, as we turned onto a broad street, he said, "This is East Hampton."

He drove slowly, so that I could savor to the full that

wide and lovely street. For a considerable distance down its center stretched a moat-like pond. Its quiet waters reflected the tall elms and fine old houses that must have been standing there when Colonials in knee breeches and scarlet-coated soldiers of King George moved along this street.

"And now," he said, "for the beaches."

A few minutes later we stood on a beach backed by high dunes. "Right here," he said, "is where a Nazi submarine landed four saboteurs one foggy night during World War Two. They came ashore in a rubber boat, together with cases of explosives to be buried for later use. A few minutes after they landed, the leader of the group not only blundered into a patrolling coast guardsman, but he was silly enough to think he could bribe the coast guardsman into silence. Within a week the whole bunch had been rounded up, without having sabotaged anything even as strategic as a brassiere factory."

He paused, and then added, "Want to take a look at Gardiner's Island? Not that we can go there. The present owner keeps armed guards to make sure no uninvited person sets foot there. But we can look at it."

We did, after driving a few miles to another beach. As I looked out over the sparkling water to the green, low-lying island, Steve Connery said, "The Gardiner family bought that island from the Indians in sixteen thirty-nine. Captain Kidd is supposed to have buried loot there, but the Gardiners say it's all been dug up. Maybe it has, or maybe they just want to discourage people from sneaking over and digging holes. Okay, let's turn around."

As we drove back along East Hampton's Main Street, he turned into the curb before a large saltbox structure of brown shingledown. "The Haylock House," he said. "Here's where we have lunch."

Surprised and hesitant, I went with him into the walnut-paneled dining room. Taking a sightseeing tour was one thing. Lunching with him at an expensive-looking restaurant was another. Even though he hadn't said so, probably he was married.

As a major-domo seated us at a white-clothed table and a waitress took our order, I kept debating how to phrase my question. "Do you and your wife live out here all year?" Of course they must, since he ran the village paper. "I'd like to buy some clothes. Where does your wife shop out here?" No, that would sound silly, too. I was sure he'd sensed that I'd have more important uses for my salary than clothes.

It wasn't until the waitress had placed fruit cups before us and turned away that I decided to ask the question directly.

"Mr. Connery—"

"Steve, for God's sake."

"Steve, are you married?"

"No, I'm a divorcé."

"A *what?*"

"Divorcé. With one e. Two e's for a divorced woman, one for a divorced man. The word isn't applied to men very often, but it's in the dictionary."

"I'm sorry."

"That I'm divorced? I'm not. I'm sorry I married her, the little leech, and I get sorrier every time I make out an alimony check. But I'm not sorry I'm divorced."

I said, feeling embarrassed warmth in my face, "Well, I'm glad you're not sorry."

He grinned. "I've got a real oldie for you. Did anyone ever tell you that you're especially pretty when you're embarrassed?"

"Not that I recall."

Nicole, I thought suddenly. Before this, I should have told him about Nicole. Anxiety tightened my nerves. If, as he appeared to be, he was attracted to me, and if that attraction had influenced his decision to hire me, he might be annoyed indeed to learn that I was not just a young widow, but a widow with a child.

Well, there was no help for it. "But it's my daughter who's going to be the real beauty. She's a brown-eyed blonde."

He laid down his spoon. "Daughter!"

"Yes, she's five now." When he said nothing, I went on wretchedly, "Do you—I mean, does that—"

With a gentleness in his voice I hadn't heard before, he said, "Were you afraid I wouldn't like the idea of your being a mother? I was just surprised, that's all."

He paused, and then asked, "You need that job pretty bad, don't you?"

"That job or some job, in the worst way."

"It's still yours. Just don't misspell any names. Now eat your fruit cup, like a good girl."

We drove back to the *Messenger* office after lunch, where I gave him my social security number and other data necessary for my employment. On a typewriter which, together with its metal stand, he and Jim hauled out from the back room, I typed two business letters, and then called a half-dozen people whose names and numbers Steve handed me. To each person who answered I gave my name, and said that I was now writing the paper's social column.

By a quarter of five, I'd typed up the information that the Clarence Hallorans planned a three-week tour of Ireland next fall, that Eileen Seaver had won a scholarship to Bennington College, that the George Hayworths had celebrated their silver anniversary with a dinner for twelve at Saginaw Inn, and that Douglas Warren, 15, was in Southampton Hospital with a broken leg.

Feeling self-conscious and proud—after all, that morning I'd had no idea I was to become a columnist—I handed Steve the sheet of yellow copy paper.

"Good," he said, after a few moments, "you didn't misspell a single name. And I'm glad you're playing it straight. The subscribers wouldn't appreciate wisecracks, not from someone who's brand-new here." He glanced at his watch. "Let's call it a day, shall we?"

I pulled the plastic hood over my typewriter. "Thanks for the job. And for that tour of the Hamptons, too."

"Oh, the tour's not finished," he said casually. "I figure we ought to see Sag Harbor this evening."

"This evening!"

"There's a restaurant at the marina there. Dancing from about nine o'clock on. Local people as well as the summer crowd go there, so I'll be able to point out some of the people you'll be writing about. How does that sound?"

It sounded wonderful. For almost eight months I hadn't had dinner with a man, or danced—

Then I thought of the Hauklids, with their obvious desire to keep the rest of the world at arm's length. If Steve Connery called for me at their house tonight, they might be very annoyed indeed.

Steve said, "What's the trouble?"

"My aunt and uncle. They're rather—standoffish."

His tone was dry. "I know."

"If you call for me at their house—"

"Then I won't. Meet me here around a quarter of eight, and we'll drive over to Sag Harbor. How will that be?"

"I think it will be just fine."

I left, then, and drove back along the highway toward the Hauklids' private road. About a quarter of a mile before I reached it, I saw a number of cars and trucks in a vacant field. Slowing as I passed, I read the words, "Haley Brothers Circus, Two Nights Only, August 25 and 26," on a white banner some denim-clad men were stretching between two aluminum posts.

As I drove on, past a field of still-unharvested potatoes, past a gas station that was nothing more than a shed, two gas pumps, and an outdoor phone booth, I found myself smiling. My mother had told me about the small traveling circuses that visited the Hamptons during her childhood and girlhood. So they still did. I'd take Nicole, who'd never seen a circus. Surely, now that I had a job, I could afford two tickets.

I turned onto the Hauklids' overgrown private road, running through its tunnel of interlaced trees. Undoubtedly my aunt and uncle would be glad I'd already found a job, since it meant they'd be rid of me that much sooner.

A sudden thought made me ease up on the gas pedal. It wasn't until I'd said I was staying with the Hauklids that Steve had offered me a job.

Was that the reason he'd offered it? Surely not. It was only that it had taken him a few minutes to realize that I might be able to hold it down. Anyway, that was what I was going to believe. I needed that job, and liked it, too much to start being uneasy about how I'd got it.

I drove on, slowing as I passed the little graveyard, and half expecting, and perhaps hoping, that I'd see a dark-haired young man inside the railed enclosure. I didn't.

Thinking of what I'd wear that night, I drove on. It really didn't require much thought. I'd brought with me only one dress, a scoop-necked beige silk jersey, which would be at all appropriate for dining out.

I heard a shot and, almost simultaneously, the sound of shattering glass.

My foot came off the gas pedal, and the engine coughed

and died. I stared at the small hole, with cracks radiating from it, in the right-hand side of the windshield.

I thought, with dazed unbelief, "Why, someone shot at me."

7

Aware of the frightened surge of my blood, I gripped the steering wheel hard and told myself, "Don't be silly. It was an accident." Somewhere nearby there was a careless or incompetent hunter—

I called out in a loud, shaken voice, "Stop that shooting!"

A bluejay's raucous cry was the only answer.

Still trembling too hard to reach for the ignition, I again stared at that hole. What if it hadn't been an accident? What if, a few yards away through the trees, someone was sighting deliberately along a rifle's barrel?

I did reach for the ignition switch then. The engine's response was an empty whine. I tried again and again, aware all the time of the pulse pounding in the hollow of my throat. Realizing that I must have flooded the engine, I finally gave up and just sat there, gripping the wheel.

"You see?" I told myself. It was an accident. If anyone had wanted to kill me, he'd have had time for a dozen shots by now. Anyway, I had no knowledge of guns. For all I knew, that windshield could have been broken by some young boy with a relatively harmless air rifle—

Some young boy. Byron. I pictured him loping back

through the woods, air rifle in hand, toward that house—that house where I'd left my little girl that morning—

It flooded through me then, a panic more acute than that of a few minutes before. I reached a shaking hand toward the ignition. Mercifully, the engine caught.

But my fear didn't slacken. I drove recklessly along the narrow, tortuous road, slowing only at the curves lest I crash into a tree. Ahead was the farmyard, thank God. I drove into it, and braked to a stop.

Nicole sat on the porch's top step, cradling an orange kitten in her arms. At sight of me she cried, "Mama," and then ran across the yard, holding the kitten against her shoulder.

On trembling legs, I got out of the car. "Don't frighten her," I warned myself.

She held the kitten up to me. "She's mine," she announced ecstatically. "Aunt Marian said so."

"That's fine, dear, but don't hold her too tightly." As Nicole trotted beside me toward the house, I asked, "Where—where is everyone?"

"Her name's Neil Armstrong. I was going to call her Punkin, but—"

"Nicole, answer my question. Where is everyone?"

"Uncle Loren and Byron are in the veg'ble garden."

"Vegetable," I corrected automatically. "Where's Aunt Marian?"

"I don't know. She just said why didn't I play out on the porch with Neil."

We'd reached the house now. "Well, why don't you stay out here for a few more minutes?"

Without answering, she sank to the porch steps and crooned, "Neil, Neil."

Perhaps later I'd try to explain that you don't name a female kitten after a man, not even a world hero. But right now I had more pressing concerns.

I went inside. Evening shadows were already gathering in the long hall. Standing just inside the door, I called, "Aunt Marian?"

No answer. Farther back along the hall the grandfather's clock gave a preliminary whir, as if clearing its bronze throat, and then struck six mellow notes.

Beyond the kitchen, clear at the end of the long hall, the back door opened and closed, and footsteps came toward me. I hurried forward, calling, "Aunt Marian?"

"Yes, Catherine."

When we came face to face, she'd already passed the rectangle of fading afternoon light that fell from the kitchen into the hall. She was carrying a white plastic laundry basket piled high with what looked like dish towels. In this light, even weaker here than near the front door, it was hard to be sure. "I nearly forgot to bring these in off the line. And whenever I do that, it's almost certain to rain." I didn't answer, and after a moment she asked sharply, "What's the matter?"

I blurted, "Someone shot at me." The trembling came back. I leaned against the wall to steady myself.

She stood motionless and silent for perhaps five seconds. "Catherine, that's absurd. Maybe you heard a shot, but—"

"There's a bullet hole in my windshield." Why had I been such a fool as to start telling her about it in this dim light? It was so hard to make out her expression. "At least I think it must have been made by a bullet, although perhaps a pellet from an air rifle—"

"Catherine, you'd better sit down."

I followed her into the kitchen and sat down on a chair beside the enamel-topped table. Crossing the room, she placed the laundry basket on the sinkboard and then drew a glass of water "Drink this." Then, a few moments later: "Draw several deep breaths. That's right. Now tell me what happened."

I told her. As I talked, I felt my nerves grow less taut, and my trembling cease. While I'd been driving so recklessly along that road, my one thought had been to get Nicole and myself far away from this place. We'd get by, somehow.

Now my panic began to seem foolish. After all, such incidents were fairly common. Back in Chicago I'd known at least three people whose car windshields had received similar damage. In none of the cases had the driver known for sure whether a bullet had caused the hole, or a pebble thrown back by the wheels of a car ahead, or the pellet from an air rifle.

Aunt Marian had been folding dish towels and putting them into a drawer. "Did you look around in the car for a bullet?"

"No, I didn't think of doing that."

"Well, probably it wasn't a real bullet. More likely it was some kid with a BB gun, hunting birds."

After a moment I asked, "Does Byron have a BB gun?"

As I'd feared, she became all maternal defensiveness. "He does not! Do you think I'd—? Besides, Byron likes birds. Not a spring passes but he brings in a young robin, or oriole, or some other bird that's fallen out of a nest. I mix up egg and cracker crumbs, and he feeds them—"

"I'm sorry, but I needed to know. I mean, there's Nicole."

Her face softened. "It's all right." Turning, she opened a second cabinet drawer and began to put away the rest of the dish towels, folding each one and smoothing it with her hand. "Did you get a job?"

"Yes, Steve Connery hired me to work on his paper. I suppose you know him."

Her reply was slow in coming. "Not really. Just to nod to when I go into the village to shop or pick up the mail. He's been here only eight years."

Eight years, in a community this small, and she knew him only to nod to. Again I wondered at the Hauklids' self-imposed isolation.

She asked, "Weren't there any other jobs?"

Did she, I wondered, have some reason for not wanting me to work for Steve Connery? "There was one at the bank, but I didn't apply for it. He said he'd pay me just as much, and I think the job's going to be fun." I paused. "He's asked me to have dinner with him tonight."

She turned to me, her face taut. "He's coming here?"

"No, no. I'll meet him in Neptague. That is, I intended to meet him. But now I feel so—"

"Why not meet him?" Evidently all she'd feared was that their sacred privacy might be further violated. "If you're worrying about Nicole, don't. I have a pile of mending, enough to keep me busy well past midnight, in that little sewing room off the living room. I'll put her to bed on the couch in there. You can take her upstairs when you come home."

"Thanks, Aunt Marian. I believe I will go." I rose. "I hope Nicole won't mind too much."

"Can't let a five-year-old run your life, Catherine; not even your own five-year-old."

"I know. Is it all right for her to bring that kitten into the house?"

"Of course."

Going out to the front porch, I said, "Come, Nicole. Time for your bath."

We climbed to the big old bathroom, where Nicole surrendered the kitten long enough for me to undress and bathe her. Then, in her pink terrycloth robe, and with Neil in her arms, she crossed beside me to the bedroom.

I said, opening a bureau drawer, "You'll have supper in your pajamas and robe tonight, darling."

"Why?"

"So Aunt Marian won't have to help you undress later. She'll be putting you to bed. You see, someone has asked me to go out for the evening." I turned to her, the small pajamas in my hand. "I'm sure you won't mind that."

The brook-brown eyes looked up at me limpidly. "I won't mind if you'll let me take Neil to bed with me."

What a shrewd little horse trader she was going to grow up to be! I had a whimisical vision of her at some international conference table thirty years from now, America's most beautiful, and tough, negotiator, offering to share the mineral rights on Mars in return for a free hand in the rest of the solar system. "If Aunt Marian says it's all right."

A deep voice called from downstairs, "Catherine!"

"Wait here a moment, darling."

I went out to the landing. At the foot of the stairs, Loren Hauklid's tall, wide-shouldered body stood silhouetted against the light coming through the open front door. "Will you come down here for a minute?"

When I'd descended the stairs, he said, "I thought you wouldn't want Nicole to hear." Reaching into the pocket of his blue denim shirt, he drew something out and held it on his palm. "Marian told me what happened as you were driving home this afternoon, so I went out and looked in your car. I found this on the floor."

I stared down at the little bullet. "What kind is it?"

"The kind you use in a twenty-two rifle." He dropped the bullet back into his pocket. "It's not too powerful, but if it hit you just right, it could have killed you, or at least blinded you."

His mouth thinned. "Used to be you had to worry about this sort of thing only in the fall, but now—Well," he added abruptly, "I'd better go out and make sure Byron's not pulling up the squash plants along with the weeds."

Turning, he walked out the front door. I stood motionless for a moment. Had he been trying to frighten me about the fact that I'd have to drive through those woods twice each working day? It was even possible that he himself had fired that bullet, although I shrank from the thought. No matter how he'd changed, surely he wouldn't endanger the life of Caroline Jessup's daughter. No, probably he hadn't fired that shot. But he might be hoping that the incident would cause me to take Nicole and myself away from there.

Well, it wouldn't. The chances were overwhelmingly against another stray bullet coming anywhere near me. I needed to stay here, and I would. And from now on, I wouldn't allow the Hauklids to make me feel intrusive. Samuel Jessup's granddaughter and great-granddaughter had a right to seek shelter in this house.

I glanced at my watch. Allowing for time to give Nicole her supper, I'd have about half an hour in which to dress for my date. Turning, I went up the stairs.

8

It was almost dark when I reached Neptague. Steve Connery sat in his car in front of the newspaper office. I parked on the opposite side of the street, hoping that in the dim light he wouldn't notice the bullet hole in my windshield. I didn't want to tell him tonight about the incident. For a few hours, at least, I wanted to forget about that old house and the people who lived there.

As I crossed the street, he got out of his car and stood holding the door open for me, a smile on his long face, and looking a very acceptable escort indeed in gray flannels, dark blue blazer, and knitted blue tie.

On the way to Sag Harbor, I told him about seeing that advertising banner for the circus. "I know," he said. "They've taken a nice big ad in the paper. Circuses are strange, especially these small traveling shows. They're fun, and yet to me there is something weird, even grotesque, about them. Have you ever felt that?"

"Come to think of it, I have."

"Perhaps they stir some racial memory of the Middle Ages. Circuses are descendants not only of the jugglers and bear-baiters who used to travel from town to town.

They also stem from those old morality plays the Church used to send around, complete with skeleton, to scare people with threats of hell and the devil.

"There's an especially grotesque aspect to these small shows. I'd heard most of the roustabouts were alcoholic derelicts. When this same circus toured eastern Long Island two years ago, I went out and watched them unload. I could see it was true. That night I went to the performance. Because the circus couldn't afford more than a couple of real clowns, they'd dressed those poor stumblebum roustabouts in sleazy yellow clown suits and painted their faces. After the show I talked to the manager, and he told me that almost all small circuses do that."

He added, "We're now in Sag Harbor."

We passed small bungalows, a park, and a large pond, dully gleaming in the last of the daylight. On its surface I could make out dull white blobs—escapees from Long Island duck farms, Steve told me—floating like oversized water lilies. Then we were moving between two lines of stately old houses.

"Captain's Row," he said, "where the sailing ship masters lived. Can you make out that railed enclosure on the roof of that house over there? Captains' wives used to go up there in hopes of catching a first glimpse of the returning fleet. Sometimes not all the whaling ships came back. That's why those railed enclosures are called widow's walks."

"The houses are so much closer together here than in the other villages."

"That's because the whaling ships were sometimes away from home as long as two years. The captains wanted their wives and children to be close to neighbors, for company and protection."

We turned left on a sloping street that ran past a handsome old building which, Steve said, was the first customhouse built in the United States. At the foot of the street stood the restaurant, a rambling structure of brown shingledown.

As we entered, I looked to my right along a softly lighted bar, and felt a sudden leap of my pulses. Philip Owen, seated there with five other people, had turned his dark head to look at us. For an instant his gray eyes held mine. Then he called, "Hello, Steve. How's the newspaper business?"

"Modestly flourishing," my companion answered. He touched my arm. "Here's someone you might like to meet."

Philip Owen and the two other men were on their feet now. Steve said, "Cathy, this in Phil Owen. Mrs. Morrel, Phil."

He said, "How do you do?" Only his eyes said, "Hello again." Well, if he had some reason for wanting it that way— I murmured an acknowledgment.

"Cathy, I'll give you three guesses. What does Phil do for a living?"

I smiled. "Wine taster? Bill collector? Mink farmer?"

"He's a history professor at Southampton College."

"I'd never have guessed it."

Philip smiled at me, and then said, "Mrs. Morrel, Steve, these are some friends of mine down from Boston."

He introduced them, starting with the girl beside him, a handsome brunette with an aquiline nose. She said, "Howja dew?" in one of those clenched-teeth finishing school accents. For some reason, I didn't like her much. I murmured greetings to her and the rest of the party. Then Steve and I went up a short flight of stairs to the dining room, with its handsome exposed beams of redwood, soft lighting, and long redwood planting boxes filled with dwarf palmettos.

When we were seated at our table, Steve said, "Nice fellow, Owen, and crazy about eastern Long Island history. He's always dropping into the *Messenger* office to look up something in the back files."

A red-haired woman, seated with several others at a table behind him, was staring at me over his shoulder. No, not staring. She was glaring, her gray-green eyes narrowed slightly, and her lips compressed. Puzzled and embarrassed, I transferred my gaze from her face to Steve's.

"Was Philip Owen raised out here?"

"No, that's the funny part. He first came out here last June, to teach summer school. And yet he's as hipped on the history of the Hamptons as if his people had lived here since before the Revolution. As a matter of fact, he wasn't even born in the United States. Somebody told me his mother brought him here when he was five years old. They were war refugees, from one of the occupied countries."

"Was his father dead?"

"I suppose so. Anyway, his mother married an American named Owen."

Our Scotch-and-sodas came just then. All through drinks and the shrimp cocktail and onion soup courses, he discreetly indicated various people in the room, and told me of their occupations, eccentricities, and approximate status in the community.

At last I said, "Don't turn around now, but there's a red-haired woman with a party at the table behind you. Do you know who she is?"

"Yes, and I don't have to turn around. I saw her when we came in. That's Edna Carson. She runs the beauty shop in Neptague. Hey, the orchestra's here."

Turning in my chair, I saw that four musicians in gray trousers and red jackets had taken their places on the small bandstand. "And here comes our scallopini," Steve added.

A waitress set covered dishes before us. When she'd gone, Steve asked, "How are you getting along at the Hauklids'?"

I lifted golden veal scallopini onto my plate. "All right. Nicole seems to like being there, and that's the main thing."

"What do you think of Loren Hauklid?"

My nerves tightened. "I scarcely know him. I'd never even met him until yesterday."

"Still, you ought to have formed some sort of opinion."

I said, aware of a growing resentment, "No, not really."

After a moment he asked, through the orchestra's first strains of "Vie en Rose," "Do those Dobermans he keeps frighten you?"

I laid down my knife and fork. "Steve, you didn't offer me a job until after I'd told you I was the Hauklids' niece. Is that why you offered it, because you're—curious about them?"

"Lord, you are mistrustful, aren't you? At lunch you were afraid I'd fire you because you hadn't told me you have a little girl. And now you think the only reason I hired you was that I want to snoop on the Hauklids."

"Maybe not the only reason. But was it one reason?"

He broke a breadstick in half, and then dropped both pieces back into the wicker basket. "All right, it was one reason."

My tone was cold. "You hoped I'd spy on my aunt and uncle for you?"

"Now that's a hell of a way to put it!" He paused, and then went on, "Okay, I'm not only curious about Loren Hauklid. I hate his guts. If it weren't for him, maybe my sister wouldn't be a widow today."

He went on to explain that two autumns ago his sister and brother-in-law had come from New Jersey to spend a few days with him. "Cliff had a new shotgun. He went onto Hauklid land to hunt pheasants. That was wrong, of course, considering that he couldn't possibly have missed all those no-trespassing signs. But still, losing his life for it was like—oh, like being executed for parking beside a fire-plug."

"What happened?"

"Cliff had rented a jeep because he hadn't wanted to drive his own car over those rough back roads. He turned off the Hauklids' private road, parked between two trees, and got out. He'd moved only a few yards when he saw these two Dobermans streaking toward him. They didn't bark or growl, but just hurtled toward him through the trees like wild animals. He managed to get back into the jeep and turn it onto the road and drive away, but he was still gasping for breath when he got back to Naptague. That night he had a heart attack, and the next morning he died in the hospital."

I said, feeling sick, "Did your brother-in-law see Loren there in the woods?"

"No, just the dogs, and as a matter of fact, Hauklid denied to me that he'd let the dogs loose. But I'll get to that later. First, I wanted to tell you that after the funeral my sister and I consulted a lawyer about taking legal action against Hauklid. The lawyer advised against it. In the first place, he said, Cliff had been trespassing. In the second place, it would be hard to prove Hauklid deliberately set the dogs on him, and even harder to establish, before a court of law, that the incident had been responsible for the heart attack, although of course it was.

"And so," he finished bitterly, "one woman's left without a husband, and three kids are left without a father."

"You say you talked to Loren?"

"Yes, about a week after Cliff's funeral. I just drove up to his house around sunset. Not even a phone call first. Hauklid himself opened the door and looked at me, deadpan."

I imagined how the two men must have looked confronting each other, there with the sunset light washing over the ugly farmyard. Loren's handsome face, probably, had been controlled, watchful, and Steve's bony one white with rage.

"Did he ask you in?"

"No. And so I just stood there on the porch and cussed him out. Finally he said he hadn't set the dogs loose that afternoon. When I asked who had, he said he didn't know. He said he'd found the dogs loose in the woods, and asked both his wife and son if they'd opened the cage door. They'd said they hadn't. Then Hauklid added something about his son not being entirely responsible, which I guess is the truth. Sometimes when Mrs. Hauklid comes into the village she brings the poor, half-witted bastard with her—"

He broke off, looking appalled. "I'm sorry."

"Because he's my cousin? Don't worry, I'm not sensitive about it. I mean, I know that retarded people crop up in all sorts of families." I paused. "And that was the last time you saw Loren?"

"It was the only time."

"The only time! But didn't you tell me you've lived in Neptague for eight years?"

"I did."

"And in all that time—"

"I'd never met him. Cathy, I think there's something wrong with him. Paranoia, maybe. He shuts the whole world out. His wife does the family shopping—all of it. She's always the one who comes to the village for mail, and to ship by railway express some sort of ceramics he makes. I don't know what they are, but the stationmaster told me the boxes go to some novelty company in New Jersey."

"He makes place card holders. I saw them."

For a few moments neither of us spoke. Could Loren be mentally ill? The expression in the deep blue eyes set in that handsome face seemed rational enough. And yet that outburst of his in the workshed had struck me as excessive—

"Another thing," Steve was saying. "People tell me he used to be your grandfather's farm manager, and that Hauklid farmed the place for a year or so after your grandfather's death. Then he quit farming, just like that. All those once-productive acres lying there—"

"He told me the reason for that. The water table's so low that he'd have to sink very deep wells in order to irrigate. And that would cost too much."

"Nonsense! Oh, some farmers do have to irrigate now. But twenty-five years ago or so, when Hauklid quit farming, growers got by with just the rainfall, or water from shallow wells. No, I think something happened to him—emotionally, or mentally, or however you want to put it. He decided to shut everyone out. And he couldn't have if he'd gone on farming. He'd have had to employ people for at least part of the year, he'd have had to negotiate contracts with wholesalers, and so on."

Perhaps he had broken down, I reflected, or at least been driven in upon himself. Certainly he'd been an unhappy man, laboring under great strain, when my mother knew him. Perhaps, after my mother left, his emotional burden had seemed all the heavier.

"Then again, maybe he's just lazy." Steve's tone was cynical. "Your grandfather must have left money as well as land. And farming's hard work. Maybe Hauklid just decided to take it easy."

I could have explained, of course, that the Hauklids had only the income from my grandfather's estate, an income too small to provide them with even a modest living. But I'd have had to give him the reason for my grandfather's act. And I didn't want to discuss my mother's sad little love affair of years and years ago, at least not with a man I'd met only that morning.

"Angry, Cathy? I mean, because I've been talking about your relatives?"

I said slowly, "No, it's better that I hear these things."

He nodded. "That's the way I figure." He added, with a frown, "In fact, I don't think you and your little girl should go on staying there. As I started to tell you this morning, I know these two young women who've taken a lease on a beautiful old house in East Hampton. They're looking for a third girl to share expenses. It would cost you a hundred a month, plus part of the food and utility bills, of course. As for your little girl, you could put her in kindergarten. The one over in North Haven is quite good, they tell me."

If I tried to meet expenses like that, I'd be no nearer accumulating a nest egg for Nicole and myself than if I'd stayed in Chicago. "No, Steve. The Hauklids are—odd, but I don't feel I'm in any danger there." Fleetingly, I though of that bullet hole in my windshield. But that, I'd already decided, had been an accident, and one very unlikely to reoccur.

I went on, "I like my aunt, and I trust her to take care of Nicole. What's more, Nicole's happy there, now that she's gotten over her first feeling of strangeness. It's an ideal arrangement."

My tone must have been firm indeed, because after a moment he smiled and said, "Your business, of course." He glanced at my almost empty plate. "Like to dance before we order dessert?"

"Very much," I said, and hoped that my tone told him I hadn't minded his giving me advice.

We danced again after dessert and coffee. We'd just returned to our table the second time when I say Philip Owen moving toward us. He said, "Steve, our party's about to leave. I wonder if I might borrow a dance with Mrs. Morrel before I go."

"That's up to Mrs. Morrel. Personally, I'd rather you

just left." His smile, apparently, was meant to indicate he was only kidding.

"Mrs. Morrel?"

I smiled and nodded. Going out onto the floor, we began to dance to a bossa nova beat.

Six years before in Philadelphia, at a large party, a young man whose name turned out to be Bill Morrel crossed the room and asked me to dance. When his hand first touched mine, I'd felt an odd electric tingle. It had startled me, because until then I'd thought that it was only in fiction that people could feel an immediate physical response to a stranger.

Something like that was happening to me again, making me feel self-conscious, awkward, and even, because of that memory of Bill, a shade guilty.

He said, smiling, "Thanks for not giving me away. It wouldn't do to have it get around that a faculty member violates no-trespassing signs."

"I suppose it wouldn't." After a moment I added, "That girl you're with, that Miss Kennedy, is very attractive."

"Kenley. Elaine Kenley."

"Oh! I suppose it was all that hair—" I broke off, appalled, and then added, "But she's very attractive."

"You said that before." He grinned, and went on, "Her brother, the rotten fink, told me that most of it's a fall. Her brother's the short, stocky one. She came down here from Boston with him, so he fixed up a date for me. A blind one, I mean. I'd never met her before."

"Oh."

"They're all going back to Boston tomorrow."

"Oh," I said again. I didn't add "Good," and I hoped my tone hadn't.

When the dance was over, he said, "Don't go back to your table for a moment." I looked at him questioningly, and he added, "Will you have dinner with me? Saturday night, say?"

I was silent for a moment, feeling both pleased and uncomfortable. Somehow it was harder to explain the situation to him than it had been to explain to Steve.

"The trouble is, my aunt and uncle are—well, perhaps reclusive is the word."

"In view of all those signs, I'd say reclusive is exactly the word." He paused. "You mean they wouldn't want my coming to their house?"

"That's it."

He smiled. "Well, I've got an idea for a perfectly wonderful dinner date. It will start in the afternoon. Right near the college there's a spot called Wild Plum Beach. You can't miss it. Will you meet me there at four o'clock Saturday afternoon?"

We'd started to move off the dance floor by then. I said, dismayed, "I promised to take my little girl to the beach Saturday afternoon."

"Well, bring her along."

"For dinner, too?"

"Why not? It'll be a beach dinner. You're not to bring even a potato chip. I grew up on the Maryland shore, so I'm an old hand at beach dinners."

"All right. Wild Plum Beach, four o'clock, Saturday."

"And bring sneakers, old ones, for both yourself and your little girl."

We'd almost reached the table, where Steve had gotten to his feet, when a hand fell on my arm. Turning, I looked into the face of the red-haired woman, Edna Carson. She was smiling, but hostility still glinted in her gray-green eyes.

"You're Miss Morrel, aren't you? I mean, Mrs. Morrel?"

"Yes."

"Could I have a word with you, in the ladies' room?"

I said wonderingly, "Why, I suppose so." Turning to Philip, I smiled and said, "Good night."

"Good night. Don't forget." He nodded to Steve, and then walked toward the bar.

I said, "Steve, will you excuse me for a moment?"

His gaze went quizzically from me to the red-haired woman and then back again. "Of course."

Following Edna Carson, I moved out of the dining room.

9

The powder room was at the end of the short hall. As we entered, a woman came out of the other section, threw a disparaging but resigned look at her reflection in the mirror behind the long dressing table, and went out into the hall.

Edna Carson said, "Let me see if there's anyone else."

While I waited, puzzled and a bit apprehensive, beside the dressing table, she went into the other section. Reappearing almost immediately, she said in a grimly purposeful tone, "Now."

My resentment flared. "Would you mind telling me how you knew my name?"

"Loren told me you'd moved in on him and Marian," she said impatiently, "and this afternoon a customer told me a Catherine Morrel had phoned her from Steve Connery's office."

"So when you saw me with Steve—"

"Look, do you mind? I want to talk fast, before somebody comes in. The main thing I want to get across is—lay off!"

I stared at her. "You mean, you have a claim on Steve Connery?"

"I'm talking about Loren Hauklid!"

Of course, I thought. The redhead with a taste for gamy literature. I wasn't particularly surprised by her identity, but by her boldness.

Then indignation sent hot color into my face. "Do you realize what you're saying? He's my aunt's husband!"

"So what? Maybe that wouldn't stop him where a pretty girl is concerned. I mean, I know Loren."

"But you don't know me! And if you think for one moment—" I broke off, aware that my voice was shaking.

She studied me, eyes narrowed. "That would really turn you off him? His being Marian's husband?"

"That, and a lot of other things. Now if that's all you had to say to me—"

"Wait. Oh, please wait!"

I turned back to her. "Well?"

"Don't tell anyone about this. Above all, don't tell Loren."

"All right."

"You've got to promise! Loren told me eight years ago, right at the start, that if I ever told anyone about us, or ever even mentioned him in any way—well, it would be over, that's all."

Wanting to get out of there, I said, "I promise," and turned toward the door. She caught my arm.

"Maybe you don't understand." No hostile suspicion in the gray-green eyes now. Just anxiety. "Loren's the most important thing in the world to me."

I said, still repelled but feeling a stir of pity, "Why have you settled for another woman's husband? Why don't you get one of your own?"

She glanced briefly at her reflection. Like the woman

who'd walked out of the powder room a few minutes before, Edna Carson looked dissatisfied with what she saw in the mirror. But she didn't look resigned. She looked frightened and unhappy.

"That might not be so easy," she said. "And anyway, I'd rather have Loren on—on these terms than be any other man's wife."

What sad, sad idiots people could make of themselves, and all in the name of love. A sentence from one of Graham Greene's books floated through my mind: "I don't think God could have been in a serious mood when he gave to mankind the sexual instinct."

I said, "I wouldn't tell anyone even if you hadn't asked me to. I don't want to get mixed up in any business of the Hauklids, I just want to get back to Chicago, as soon as I can."

She nodded. "That's good. That house is no place for you."

Without saying good night, I went out into the hall. As I moved toward the dining room, her last sentence echoed in my mind. It seemed to me now that the words could have carried a threat.

She was an impulsive, emotional, and unhappy woman. Could it have been she out there in the woods this afternoon with a rifle in her hand, hoping to frighten me away from the Hauklid place?

No, I decided, that would have been the act of a devious person. And there'd been nothing sly about her behavior tonight. Instead, she displayed her jealousy and fear with an almost childlike directness.

Steve rose as I approached the table. "And what was that all about?"

I said, thinking rapidly, "Just a misunderstanding."

"About what?"

"Maybe I should have said a case of mistaken identity. She thought I was someone who'd charged a permanent at her shop last year, and never paid for it."

"I hope you convinced her."

"I did."

"Would you like more coffee, or do you want to go?"

"It's getting late. I think we'd better go."

As we descended the steps from the dining room to the entrance, I looked to my left along the bar. Philip Owen and his party were no longer there.

Emerging from the restaurant, we found that a strong wind had sprung up, driving wispy clouds across the starlit sky, and stirring the branches of maples and horse chestnuts along Captain's Row. No ghostly white blobs floated on the pond's ruffled surface now. Evidently the ducks had decided that tonight they'd sleep more restfully in the tall reeds at the pond's edge.

When we drew up before the darkened *Messenger* office, I said, "Thank you for a pleasant evening, Steve. I feel I'm really getting to know the Hamptons."

"You haven't seen some of them yet. Westhampton, for instance. There's a summer theater there. How about our going next Saturday?"

"I can't. I'm sorry, Steve."

He drummed his fingernails on the steering wheel for a few seconds, and then asked lightly, "A date with Phil Owen?"

"Yes. I'm sorry."

"Don't be. We can go some other time. Besides, I'm too old for you. Too experienced, anyway."

"I'm not inexperienced. I was married for six years. I have a child."

"From the look of you, those were good experiences. There are other kinds. Anyway, as I said, don't be sorry. I've found me a good speller, and good spellers are rarer than attractive dates, these days. Now shall I follow you home? That private road must be dark as pitch at night, especially when there's no moon."

I glanced across the street toward my little car. It stood in a pool of wind-stirred shadow under a giant maple. Probably, when he accompanied me across the street, he wouldn't notice that bullet hole in my windshield. But if he followed me clear to the Hauklid farmyard, he might very well notice. And then he'd start insisting that I leave there.

"No, please don't come with me. If they heard two cars, they might be—upset."

"Just as you say."

He walked with me across the street to my car. He opened the car door, cupped my chin with his other hand, and kissed me lightly. "Good night. Try to be on time tomorrow, huh? I want you to hold the fort while I'm out hustling ads."

"I'll be on time. Good night, Steve."

Quickly I slipped into the car, turned the ignition key, and moved away from the curb. In the rear-view mirror I saw him slowly crossing the street toward his car. It seemed to me that his shoulders slumped a little. Had he been more upset than he appeared to be about my date with Philip Owen? I hoped not, because I liked my garrulous boss, and felt grateful to him.

Once out of the village, I drove through the increasingly windy dark down a road that ran past potato fields and an occasional house. Eventually I turned left onto the highway which, half a mile farther on, bordered the Hauklid acres. I passed the white cloth banner advertising the circus. Bellying out like a ship's sail, it strained at the metal posts which held it.

As I turned onto the tunnel-like private road, a seething sound enveloped me, almost as if I were indeed in a thin-walled tunnel running under a bay, with storm-lashed water roaring all around me. It was the wind, of course, lashing the trees that walled the narrow road and interlaced their branches above it. The agitated leaves, showing white in the car's headlights and then darkening as they slipped past me, suggested flecks of foam.

Like many people, I am disquieted by a high wind. But before I'd been on that road a minute, I felt something stronger than disquiet. That steady seething, and the branchlets that whipped out toward the car windows like seeking arms rasped my every nerve. I kept telling myself that this was different from this afternoon, when a bullet's shattering impact had given me ample reason for alarm. There was no reason now. On a dark night of strong wind and lashing branches, no one would be prowling through the trees. And yet, more than ever before, I felt that these woods, fleetingly illuminated by my headlights and then slipping into pitch blackness, held menace. Some evil, biding its time, patient and implacable, had taken possession of this land, and of the house where the Jessup girls had spent their happy and uneventful girlhood.

The house. Nicole.

My senseless alarm had its way with me then. Just as I had that afternoon, I pressed down on the accelerator. I slowed at the curves, but otherwise I kept going, even when branchlets slapped across the windshield, momentarily obscuring my vision. I made five turns, six, and then I was braking to a stop in the farmyard.

Getting out, I slammed the car door. Barking erupted at the side of the house, only to cease when Loren Hauklid, probably in his workshed, called in his deep voice, "Quiet out there!" Running across the yard, I seized the screen door's handle. Aunt Marian had left the screen and the door beyond it unlatched. In the hall I saw that the living room was dark. There was diffused light, though, filtering out from some room beyond.

Swiftly I crossed the living room and halted in the sewing room doorway. Aunt Marian raised a startled face from the pillow slip she was darning. On a couch against one wall Nicole slept peacefully, with a pink blanket covering her, and the kitten curled into an orange ball at her feet.

My aunt whispered, "What is it?" Then, rising: "We'd better not talk here. We might wake her."

Moving past me into the living room, she switched on the pewter lamp. I sat down beside her on the Victorian sofa, still shaken, but beginning to feel a little foolish.

She asked, in a low but sharp voice, "What's the matter?"

"Nothing really. Driving home along that private road I just went into a panic. Maybe it was because of that stray bullet this afternoon, but I think it was mainly the wind that upset me. Anyway, I had a sudden conviction that something had happened to Nicole."

"It hasn't." Some of the tension went out of her face. "She's fine, as you saw."

"I know. It was silly." I paused, and then blurted out, "But there is something wrong with this place, and something wrong with you. What is it?"

She said, in a mechanical voice, "Something wrong with me?"

"Yes! You're afraid."

"Afraid?"

"Please don't keep—listen, Aunt Marian. I heard you phoning the college about Philip Owen this morning. I didn't mean to eavesdrop. It was an accident. Now why would you check up on him if you weren't—afraid of something?"

Her face had paled momentarily, but now a spot of color appeared on each cheekbone. "Don't I have a right to check up on people who trespass? I was born on this land, remember."

"Yes, but when I told you about him, you made no indication that you were going to check up."

She said, after a moment, "I didn't think of doing it then. It was only after you went for a walk that I thought of it."

My aunt was a bad liar. But that, of course, didn't mean that I would get the truth out of her.

She went on, in that heckling manner with which people sometimes try to mask their native timidity, "And anyway, I shouldn't think you'd want strangers walking into the family cemetery. Those are your ancestors, too, you know."

"I know."

"What's more, this land will be half yours someday." Pain crossed her face, and I knew she was thinking of how the bank my grandfather had named as trustee would undoubtedly order the house and land sold, so that the estate could be divided. Perhaps she was thinking, too, of how the trustees would have to go on managing Byron's share for him.

"I'm sorry, Aunt Marian."

She smiled. "That's all right. How was your date?"

Edna Carson's face, hostile and anxious, appeared before my mind's eye. Again I wondered if my aunt knew about Edna. Well, she'd never know from me.

"I had a lovely time. What's more, we ran into Philip Owen, in the restaurant where we had dinner. I have a date with him next Saturday. A cookout, at the beach. He won't be coming here. Nicole and I will meet him."

"That's probably better, considering how Loren feels." I'd been watching her as I mentioned Philip, and I'd seen no flicker of alarm in her eyes. Apparently she'd satisfied herself that he was no one to fear.

"By the way," she said, "you'll need a front door key. I put one on your bureau."

"Thank you." I rose. "Well, I'd better put Nicole to bed. And myself, too."

Going back to the sewing room, I lifted Nicole to a sitting position, took her pink robe from a chairback, and fed her arms into the sleeves. Still more asleep than awake, she climbed beside me up the stairs, with the kitten cradled in her arms.

10

The next morning I purposely arrived in Naptague half an hour early. Driving to the far end of Main Street, I turned in beside the gas pumps of Pete's Garage and Service Station. A fat, balding man, perhaps Pete himself, came out of the station house.

"How many?"

"Fill the tank, please. And could you install a new windshield for me?"

"Somebody been gunning for you, huh?" His tone was facetious.

I said, in the same tone, "Looks like it."

"I'll bet it happened on one of those back roads. Some kid with a twenty-two. It's bad enough now, but during the hunting season—! Why, you couldn't pay me to go into the woods in November."

"How long will it take to put in a new windshield?"

"Oh, I can put it in today. My supplier in Riverhead is sending over some stuff late this morning. I'll tell him to send a windshield, too."

"How much will it cost?"

"Oh, around a hundred and five."

I winced. Well, thank heaven my insurance would pay for part of it. Leaving my car there, I walked back along Main Street. I was waiting on the *Messenger's* doorstep when Steve Connery drove up.

During the next two days I took classified ads over the phone, and tried to sort out the jumbled bills and old letters in Steve's filing cabinet, and typed an editorial blast at the village trustees which, with considerable relish, he dictated to me. I also wrote, for my column, brief accounts of two birthday parties, and perhaps twenty visits by subscribers' friends and relatives. I even covered a wedding at the Methodist Church. The work was fun, and absorbing, but again and again as I typed, or searched through those messy files, I found myself thinking ahead to Saturday, and hoping it wouldn't rain.

Perhaps my employer sensed how often Philip was in my thoughts. Certainly there was a subtle change in his own manner toward me. He remained talkative and friendly, but with no hint of gallantry. He didn't mention taking me out again. And on Friday, when I returned to the office from that church wedding, I found him winding up a phone conversation with someone he addressed as "doll." Feeling a relief only slightly tinged with feminine pique, I gathered that he'd made a date for the following night.

It didn't rain Saturday. I spent the morning and early afternoon doing personal laundry, and helping Aunt Marian with housework. Around three, I dressed Nicole and myself in bathing suits, covered by flowered shifts. Then, while Byron stood wistfully by, I loaded towels, sweaters, tennis shoes, and my daughter into the little car. As we drove out of the farmyard, Nicole looked back. "Why couldn't Byron go with us?"

"He wasn't invited, dear. We'll take him another time."

"Is that why you wouldn't let me take Neil Armstrong?"

"No, it was because cats don't like the beach."

I found Wild Plum Beach easily enough. It was on a bay, at the foot of a road running off Old Montauk Highway. When we drove up onto the hard-packed sand at the edge of the beach, the only other vehicle parked there was a flat-bed truck. Its driver, loading a bushel basket filled with clams onto the truck, nodded to us, got behind the wheel, and drove off. Alighting from the car, I saw why this beach was unpopular with swimmers. I saw, too, why Philip had advised bringing sneakers. Beyond a narrow stretch of coarse sand lay tidal flats, strewn with glistening shells and rocks. On the farthest narrow ribbon of sand, separated from its neighbor by a channel of sparkling water, were perhaps twenty sea gulls, some standing motionless, some shifting restlessly, like street-corner pedestrians waiting for the green light.

Nicole had left the car to stand beside me. "It's not like that other beach." I knew she meant the Lake Michigan beach to which Bill and I had taken her the summer before. "It's better!'

It was. I stood there, savoring the solitude, and a red-sailed catboat heeling in the breeze far out of the blue water, and the way the gulls, as if at some prearranged signal, all rose on powerfully beating wings, hovered for a moment, and then settled back on the sandbar.

The sound of an engine. I turned around. Philip Owen parked a dark green station wagon beside my own car. He got out, thin and lithe in blue jeans and a faded blue shirt. "So you made it." Then, to my daughter: "Hi, Nicole."

He'd heard her name only once, and yet he'd remembered it. That must have pleased her as much as it did me. She answered "Hi!" in a tone far friendlier than she usually used with strange adults.

"How do you like this place?"

I said, "We both like it fine."

"Since you approve, let's start carrying things down to the sand."

He opened the station wagon's tailgate. Standing beside him, I looked in at cardboard boxes filled with bulging paper bags, and at an aluminum steak grill, and thermos bottles, and a bag of charcoal, and an ice chest of some sort of green plastic. "Are you sure this isn't an army field kitchen?"

He said, hauling out a long rake with curved teeth, "Nothing here that isn't needed for a well-appointed beach dinner."

"Even the rake?"

"It's a clam rake. I though we might dig a few." Leaning the rake against the car, he reached into one of the boxes and hauled out a small glass-and-rubber face mask, with a snorkel tube attached. "This is for you," he said, and handed it to Nicole. "It's the smallest I could find."

She asked, "What is it?"

"It's for lying on your stomach and looking down into the water. Air comes through this tube. Like the idea?"

She said, in a dubious tone, "Maybe."

"Well, we can try it. I brought masks for your mother and me, too."

Leaving the food and cooking equipment behind, we carried beach paraphernalia down to the sand, and spread a blanket. Nicole and I took off our beach shifts, Philip stripped to bathing trunks, and we all three put on tennis sneakers. For a while we wandered over the tidal flats, with the black, bettle-shaped shells of baby mussels and the pale, fluted ones of sea scallops grating beneath our feet. Nicole ran from tidal pool to tidal pool, hunkering down to admire tiny fish and hermit crabs, and then dashing to another pool for more moments of rapt contemplation.

At last Philip said, "Want to get some clams now? I didn't bring a rake for you. You'd find it too heavy to use. But probably you can clam with your feet."

"With my feet!"

"Yes. Many of the clams lie just under the surface of the sand. When you feel one through the soles of your sneakers, you can reach down and pick it up."

He added, "I'm afraid you can't help us, Nicole. You'd be in over your head."

Squatting beside a pool, she looked up. "I like it here better," she said, and went back to staring at the fish.

A few minutes later Philip waded out into the water, trailing a rope. The other end of the rope was attached to a half-bushel basket, set inside an inflated inner tube. I waded after him, glad of the protection my sneakers afforded against the stones and jagged shells underfoot. When he was about waist-deep, he set to work. His hunch was good. At least a third of the time, the dripping rakefuls of sand and gravel he brought up also contained clams.

As for me, I reaped a rich harvest of rocks, shells of long-departed clams, and a kind of giant sea snail which Philip said was called a whelk. At last, though, I brought up a six-inch, living clam that turned out to be the largest of the day. After that my feet in the thin-soled old sneakers seemed to have learned to distinguish between a clam's texture and a rock's. I found at least a dozen clams. When we finally waded toward shore, the basket was half full.

"We'll have a few small clams for our first course. I brought a clam knife, and one of those plastic-topped bottles of sauce."

"I'll just bet you did."

"Why don't you take the rest of the clams home with you? I'll put them in your car. That is, if you think your aunt would like to have them."

I thought of her darning pillow slips, and bartering eggs at the store in Neptague. "She'd like to."

Nicole, we learned, had definitely decided against wearing her face mask. Leaving her busy with a battered old sand pail and shovel—Aunt Marian's contribution to our outing—Philip and I waded a few yards out into the bay. "Here ought to be about right." He buckled my face mask, then his own. "Like this," he said, his voice sounding hollow through the glass, and launched himself face down on the water's surface. So did I.

Another world down there. A world where golden sunlight, striking through the water, wavered as if it, too, were liquid. A world of tiny fragments of white or red coral, and little crabs like bits of scuttling lapis lazuli, and schools of fingerlings that swirled in silver clouds. There was seaweed, too, languorously waving streamers of amber and translucent green.

Fingers touched my own, tightened around them. For several minutes I floated like that, my hand clasped by Philip's, my body gently rocked by the water, my eyes delighted by that swaying, darting, scuttling world down there. I thought, "It's like a dream, or like listening to some of Debussy's music."

He stood up finally, and so did I. We smiled at each other. For a fleeting moment I felt a return of that faint guilt, that sense that in enjoying this man's touch I was somehow betraying Bill. "It's getting late," Philip said. "We'd better dry off."

We sat on the beach blanket while our suits dried in the cooling air. Nicole, who'd abandoned her sand pail and shovel and returned to the tidal flats, kept running up with shells and brightly colored pebbles for us to admire. The tide had turned now. Already the outermost flat, where the sea gulls had stood, was covered. When the water and the still-exposed inner flats began to glisten with sunset colors—pink and pale gold and mauve—I called Nicole, put her beach shift on her, and pulled mine over my head. All three of us went back to the car for the cooking equipment, and for the sweaters we'd soon need.

Besides the clams, which Nicole refused to eat, we had steak that night, and cole slaw in cardboard containers, and corn roasted in its husks on the charcoal fire. There was lemon soda for Nicole, and a bottle of Burgundy for Philip and me. By the time he'd poured coffee from a thermos, the sky was beginning to darken. No stars were visible as yet, but in the west the thinnest possible sliver of new moon hung in the sky.

I said reluctantly, "We'd better go soon."

Disappointment came into his face. "I thought we'd build a fire, and sit beside it for a while. I brought some wood, and there's more here on the beach."

"It sounds wonderful, but Nicole should be in bed soon."

He looked over to where she sat on the sand, dropping shells and pebbles she'd collected into the tin pail. He said, in a low voice, "There's a tarp up in the station wagon, and a couple of more blankets. I could fix up a temporary bed for her here, close to the fire."

Despite the softness of his tone, she'd heard. She got up, knocking over the sand pail, ran to me, and threw her arms around my neck. "Let me, Mama; let me."

I said, after a moment, "Well, I suppose it would be all right, for an hour or so."

I didn't wrap Nicole into her cocoon of blankets until after we'd built the fire. While I sat there, listening to Philip talk of his work at the college, I kept glancing at my daughter. For perhaps ten minutes she stared at the crackling flames, at the sparks which mounted straight upward into the windless dark. Then her eyelids drooped, and finally closed.

I said to Philip, "Had you always planned to teach history?"

"Ever since I was fifteen or so."

"Was your father a teacher?"

"No, a Lutheran minister. He died when I was five."

I hesitated, and then said, "Steve Connery mentioned that you and your mother came here as war refugees."

He threw a piece of driftwood on the fire. "That's right. It was all pretty rugged. I can remember a lot of it. People with unsettled childhoods can usually remember a long way back. But I don't feel like talking about it right now." He turned his dark face toward me. "Do you mind?"

"Of course not."

After a moment he said, "How do you like being out here on eastern Long Island?"

"Long Island's fine, and my job's fine, but I don't like living with my aunt and uncle very much."

"Why not?"

"I don't like Loren Hauklid. And my aunt's unhappy and—well, strange."

"She didn't happen to call the college about me the other morning, did she?"

I felt embarrassed warmth in my face. "How did you find out?"

"The switchboard operator told me some woman had called to ask if a man of my name and description was on the faculty. I couldn't think who it might have been. Then I realized that perhaps you'd told the Hauklids about my trespassing, and they'd wanted to check up on me."

"That was it. But now she seems convinced that you're exactly what you say you are." After a moment I added lightly, "You are, aren't you? I mean, you're not a government agent looking for evidence of tax evasion, are you, or someone with an old map that says there's buried treasure on that land?"

He smiled, and then said quietly, "I'm a teacher, and I've never been anything else. First I taught at N.Y.U., where I received my bachelor's and master's degrees, and then I came out here. But I'm sorry your aunt was upset."

"Probably no one else would have been. But she seems to be in a chronic state of anxiety, even fear, although she denied that she is." I gave a little laugh. "I've felt frightened myself a couple of times."

His shoulders tensed. "Frightened?"

I hesitated, and then said with a rush, "Somebody fired a bullet through my windshield on that private road last Wednesday."

His face swung toward me. "A bullet?"

"Yes. Some careless hunter, I suppose, and it didn't come within a foot of me. But I was pretty—shook up."

"Catherine, listen to me. Leave that place."

It was odd, I reflected, that with the exception of Byron, everyone seemed to want me out of that house—my aunt, my uncle, Edna Carson, Steve Connery, and now Philip.

"I can't leave." Briefly, I told him how broke I was, and why. "Perhaps it's not so frightening to have no savings when you're on your own. But with a child to raise—well, I want to accumulate a backlog."

He took my two hands in his. "Would you let me loan you a thousand or so, so that you and Nicole wouldn't have to stay there? I *am* all on my own, with no great expenses, and a pretty good salary. The money's just sitting there in the bank. You'd have as long as you needed to pay it back."

"Thank you, but I couldn't do that."

"No," he said slowly, releasing my hands, "I suppose you couldn't." After a moment he added, "But will you let me do one thing? Follow you down that side road when you go home? I won't actually drive up to the house, if you think that would upset the Hauklids."

"Thank you. I'd be glad of the company."

For perhaps a minute we both stared into the fire. Then he said, "What was your husband like? Or is that something you don't want to talk about?"

"No, I can talk about him," I said, feeling surprised that I could. I'd never wanted to until now, in all the months since his death. "Bill was big and blond, and he was always concocting wild schemes for us, such as chartering a houseboat and going up the Amazon, or taking a trip by dog sled in Alaska. He knew we'd never do them, at least not for years and years, but he liked to talk about them. Nothing ever seemed to make him really angry except deliberate cruelty. Once the bachelor across the hall left his German shepherd alone for two days. We could hear the poor thing barking and whining and scratching at the door. The superintendent refused to go in, and so Bill jimmied the lock, and took the dog out for a walk, and fed him. When the dog's owner came back, Bill gave him such a tongue-lashing that he didn't even ask us to pay for the lock.

"He made up a continuing story for Nicole about a globe-trotting chipmunk, and told her a new episode each night at bedtime. And he was always doing nice, unexpected things. When I woke up on the morning of our anniversary, our last anniversary, there was a rose on my pillow—"

A band tightened around my throat, shutting off words. From deep inside me, sobs welled up. I put my hand over my mouth to stifle them.

Philip's arms went around me. "You won't wake her. She's sound asleep. Let it out. Let it all out."

I did, against his shoulder. The grief and loneliness I'd held in check during all those months my mother lay in the hospital gushed out of me in tears and great sobs. But when my crying was over, I felt strangely at peace.

Freer, too. It was as if, in letting my grief for Bill gush forth, I'd found a new strength to live in the present, and to make the best possible life for us, the two he'd had to leave.

Philip thrust a large white handkerchief into my hand. I straightened up, blew my nose, wiped tears from my face. For a while we were both silent, looking at little blue flames that licked along the satiny driftwood. Then I said, somewhat hoarsely, "Thanks."

"Don't mention it."

"Philip—"

"Yes?"

"How is it that you haven't married?"

"I almost did, last winter. The trouble was, I'd already made up my mind that if I could, I'd leave New York University and take an appointment at Southampton. I'd spent several weeks out here the previous summer, and I liked what I'd seen of the Hamptons."

"Your girl didn't approve?"

"No. She liked New York—she had a good job there as a fashion writer—and besides, she couldn't understand why a man would leave an old and quite well-known university for a college that had been founded only a few years before. I tried to explain that I liked the rural atmosphere, and the idea of helping shape the future of a new institution. She still couldn't go for it, and so finally we decided that our life styles, as the sociologists say, just weren't suited."

"I see."

I could understand why the girl might consider his decision impractical. Still, if she'd loved him enough—

For a while we went on looking into the fire. Then he said, "Catherine?"

I turned toward him. He must have read assent in my face, because he kissed me, his lips warm and firm against mine. When he raised his head, I saw in his face, one thin cheek illuminated by the flickering firelight, an odd expression, both tender and deeply troubled. He kissed me again, a more prolonged kiss, this time.

Abruptly he released me. "You'd better get Nicole home."

"Yes."

"I'll carry her up to your car. Then I'll come back and put out the fire."

About half an hour later, I turned onto the Hauklids' private road. Perhaps aroused by the car's motion over the rougher surface, Nicole lifted her cheek from the backrest and twisted around within the confines of the seat belt Philip had buckled around her.

"Where are we, Mama?"

"Almost home."

And we'd get there safely. For me, no demonic force prowled these woods tonight, not with the trees standing almost motionless in the calm air, not with Philip's headlights always visible in the rear-view mirror.

We were about fifty yards from the farmhouse clearing when he gave his horn a light tap. I stopped my car, and he got out and walked over to its open window.

"There's a good place to turn around back there, so I'll leave you now."

"All right. Thanks for escorting us home, and—thanks for everything."

He glanced past me to where Nicole sat turning small fists in her eyes. "I'll be correcting themes tomorrow, and

I have a faculty meeting the next night. But may I call you Tuesday at the newspaper office?"

"Of course." Tuesday, I realized, was the first night of the circus. Perhaps he'd take both Nicole and me. Since the circus was so close, I'd be able to take her home to bed after the performance, and then rejoin Philip.

"Good night, Catherine. Good night, Nicole."

My drowsy daughter and I drove into the farmyard, where I unbuckled her seat belt and set her on the ground. When I closed that balky car door, the Dobermans gave only a few token barks. Perhaps in time they'd get used to that particular sound. With the key my aunt had given me, I opened the front door and led Nicole up to our room. Neil Armstrong had already retired for the night, on my daughter's small bed. I had to move the ball of sleeping orange fluff aside so that Nicole could straighten out her legs.

When I'd hooked the door and turned off the light, I crossed to the window. The fireflies were there again, winking on and off as they drifted through the trees on the opposite side of the clearing.

The poachers were back, too, or whatever person or persons it was who moved through the swamp at night. I'd ask my aunt whether or not Jethro's Hole was dangerous. If she said it wasn't, someday I might go over and look at that swamp named after my eighteenth-century ancestor.

Turning, I moved past Nicole's bed to my own.

11

Three o'clock Sunday dinner at the Hauklids' turned out to be a strained affair. Byron was in disfavor. Ten minutes before we sat down at the table, it had been discovered that he'd broken two china eggs in the henhouse, and his luminous gray eyes still brooded over the scolding he'd received. Nicole, perhaps reacting to the uncomfortable atmosphere, grew restless and too talkative, and finally upset her milk on the tablecloth. Aunt Marian told me not to worry about it, but I could see that both she and her husband were annoyed. And when Byron began to giggle, they turned on him, transferring to their son the irritation they felt with my daughter. "No TV for you this afternoon," Loren told him.

After I'd helped with the dishes, I took Nicole upstairs for her nap. With Byron sulking in his room, my daughter asleep, Loren off in his workshed, and my aunt returned to her interminable mending, the house held an oppressive silence. Without consulting my aunt, I decided I'd go over to Jethro's Hole. Last night I'd feared the swamp might hold dangerous snakes, but today I'd recalled one of the numerous bits of information given to me by my loquacious boss: there were no poisonous snakes on Long Island. Besides, I wouldn't go into the swamp, but just to its edge.

Slipping out of the house, I walked a few yards down the private road, and then struck off to my right through the trees, toward the area where I'd seen the flickering light. Soon the ground began to slope downward. The trees grew taller and thicker, so that I moved through a deepening twilight. When the earth felt spongy beneath my feet, I halted. Ahead, black water spread around the roots of trees and around low hummocks matted with vegetation. Disliking the dim light and the fetid smell of wet and decaying plants, I turned to retrace my steps.

Objects over to my left, half concealed by a group of young swamp maples, caught my eye. I moved closer. A rubber tarpaulin had been spread out on the ground. Neatly lined up on it were a large shovel and a smaller one, a pair of hip-length rubber boots, a lantern, a coil of rope, and a big steel hook that probably weighed at least ten pounds. I'd seen pictures of such objects. They were called grappling hooks.

Poachers' equipment? For all I knew, it could be. Perhaps the hunters sank traps beneath the water for muskrats, and then drew them up with the grappling hook. As for the shovels, I couldn't see what use they would be to someone hunting illegal game, but then, I knew little of such matters.

Again I became aware of the semi-twilight, and the swamp's odor of decay. I hurried toward the road, deliberately turning my mind to the most pleasant topic I could think of—Philip Owen, and the phone call I'd receive from him next Tuesday.

As it turned out, I wasn't at the office on Tuesday to receive that call. On Monday afternoon, as soon as I'd stepped from the gray and humid out-of-doors into the house, Aunt Marian called from the living room, "That you, Cathy? There's a letter for you there on the hall table. I picked it up at the post office today."

It had been forwarded, in care of my aunt, from Chicago. Its return address was that of Grace Halliday, the Philadelphia woman whose apartment my mother had moved into after my marriage. Opening the letter, I read:

Dear Cathy,

I do so hate to bother you with this, at a time when you have other burdens. But I must. You see, now that your dear mother is gone, I've decided to give up this apartment. I'm moving down to Pensacola on August 27th to be near my daughter, whose husband is stationed at the Navy base there.

My problem is, what shall I do with your mother's things? The few pieces of furniture she had were nice, but they weren't family heirlooms, and so I don't imagine you'd want them. I can sell them if you like, and send you the money. As for her clothes, I imagine you'd like me to give them to some charity.

It's this cedar chest of hers that bothers me. I haven't opened it, although the keys are here, because I know that she kept family mementos and other things of a personal nature in that chest. I feel it's your place, rather than mine, to go through the chest and decide what should be kept.

Will you please write to me, airmail, immediately? I have so many other matters to attend to that I'd appreciate having this settled as soon as possible.

If you like, I can ship the chest to you. But one of the bottom boards was damaged when your mother had it moved to this apartment. To ship it safely, I'd have to call someone in to crate it, and you know what that sort of thing costs these days! Anyway, I'll do nothing until I hear from you.

I want to tell you again how deeply I sympathize with

you and your little girl in your double loss, and how often I hope things are going as well with you as possible.

Affectionately,
Grace Halliday.

Dismayed, I lifted my eyes from the paper and stared at the wall. August twenty-seventh was only three days away. She'd been waiting for more than a week now to hear from me. What must she have thought of my silence?

The only fair thing to do was to go down there tomorrow, and take the whole matter off her hands—sell those few pieces of furniture, phone some charity to call for my mother's clothes, and go through that cedar chest.

How far away was Philadelphia? Probably not much more than two hundred miles. I wouldn't try to make the round trip in one day, of course. I'd stay at Mrs. Halliday's apartment tomorrow night, trying to be as little bother as possible, and start driving back early the next morning.

My aunt came out into the hall. "Bad news?"

"Not really. Upsetting, that's all." I told her the contents of Mrs. Halliday's letter. "I'd better drive down there tomorrow, and come back on Wednesday."

She frowned. "It's not the best weather for driving. The radio says there's a hurricane off the Florida coast. The muggy weather we've got right now, the announcer said, is being pushed ahead of the storm. Of course, it may veer off into the Atlantic—"

"Even if it turns northwest, the chances are we won't get more than the fringes of it. Certainly I don't feel it gives me an excuse to leave Mrs. Halliday in the lurch." I paused. "May I phone her? As soon as I'm finished, I'll ask the operator for the charges, and pay you."

"All right," she said. But from her reluctant tone I could tell that a Hauklid phone bill with a long-distance charge on it would be an almost unprecedented phenomenon.

I called Mrs. Halliday, who sounded vastly relieved at hearing from me. "But wouldn't it be less—painful for you if I gave your mother's clothing away? Perhaps a simple phone call to the Lighthouse for the Blind might do it. I know that was her favorite charity."

"Thank you. I'd much rather you did it. But if you run into any difficulties, I'll take care of it when I get down there."

"A secondhand dealer is coming to look at my furniture tomorrow morning. If he offers me a fair price for your mother's furniture, shall I take it? Then all you'd have to do is go through that chest."

"I hate to put you to that extra trouble—"

"No trouble, since he'll be coming here anyway. The only bothersome aspect was not knowing what you wanted me to do. I mean, after all, your dear mother's things—"

"It was wonderful of you to feel that way about it," I cut in swiftly. Mrs. Halliday was a nice woman, but a compulsive chatterer, even over long distance. "Thank you again, and I'll see you sometime tomorrow afternoon."

When I'd hung up, I called the operator to learn the charges, and then handed sixty-five cents to my aunt. Apparently to make sure that the money wouldn't be spent for something else, she placed the coins, sealed into an envelope, in the drawer of the telephone table.

I said, "About Nicole. Mrs. Halliday didn't invite me to bring her, and I'd hate to just show up with her, considering how much the poor woman has to do."

"She'll be all right here. I'll sleep in your room tomorrow night, so that she won't be lonely."

"That would be wonderful. If she has you and Neil Armstrong, she probably won't miss me at all."

Leaning forward, I kissed my aunt's thin cheek.

12

The next morning was as gray and humid and breathlessly hot as the afternoon before. Perhaps partly because of the weather, Nicole made more fuss than I'd expected her to over the prospect of my remaining away overnight. By the time I'd soothed her down, with reminders that she'd have both Aunt Marian and the kitten in the room with her, and promises that I'd bring her a present from Philadelphia, it was well past eight o'clock. I caught up my suitcase, which was empty except for a nightgown and robe and a toothbrush, draped my hooded raincoat over my arm, and hurried out to the car.

At eight-thirty, soon after I'd turned off the Hauklids' road onto the highway, I switched on my car radio to hear the news. Because the tropical storm had turned northwestward, the announcer said, a hurricane watch was in effect from South Carolina to Cape May. However, it was a fairly slow-moving storm, and wouldn't affect the Northeast for at least another twelve hours, if then.

In Southampton, I stopped to phone the university. Mr. Owen was in class, the switchboard operator told me. I left a message with her, explaining that I'd been called to

Philadelphia, and wouldn't be back until Wednesday. Hanging up, I called my employer, who said, "Oh, hell! I was going to send you over to interview the women who are running the Clam Pie Festival in Springs. They've taken a nice big ad this year." His tone became wheedling. "They're an interesting bunch of women—TV and movie and musical comedy actresses, painters, people like that. They might even give you a couple of clam pies."

I remained firm. "Okay," he sighed, "have a good trip."

I drove on, through traffic that thickened steadily. It was almost noon when I turned onto the Verrazano-Narrows Bridge which links Long Island with Staten Island and New Jersey.

As I moved along the New Jersey Turnpike, with desolate, polluted marshland on one side of me and oil refineries belching sulpfurous smoke on the other, rain began to fall. I turned on the radio. Although still well out to sea, the storm continued to move in a northwesterly direction, and, had picked up both strength and speed. Heavy rain and high winds, now battering Virginia and Maryland, were expected to reach the northeastern states early in the evening, to be followed by clearing weather around midnight. Good, I thought. Unless the storm knocked down trees or flooded highways, I'd have no trouble driving back to Long Island the next day.

The rain grew heavier after I took the turnoff to Philadelphia but it was still of only normal summer-storm proportions when I stopped before Mrs. Halliday's apartment house, a dignified Georgian structure of red brick on a sycamore-lined street.

She met me at her apartment door, a plump little woman, hatted and gloved for the street. "Oh, I'm so glad you're here! I was just going to ask the superintendent to let you in. Do you know what's happened? I've lost a crown off a tooth, and I've had to make a four o'clock appointment with my dentist. Right now, of all times, when I have a million things to do. And on top of that, maybe we're in for a hurricane."

By that time, I'd moved with her across a living room barren of furniture. Still talking, she led me down a short hall, and stopped in the doorway of what had been my mother's bedroom. Now it held only her cedar chest and a folding cot, made up with sheets and a blanket.

"That dealer bought all her furniture, and so I put that cot— Oh, that reminds me." Opening her calfskin handbag, she extracted a check and held it toward me. "I had it made out to you. I think I got a rather good price, don't you?"

I set down my suitcase to take the check. It was a good price, I saw—more than I'd thought my mother's furniture would bring, but before I could tell her so, she rushed on, "A man from the Lighthouse picked up her coats and dresses this morning. That leaves just the chest. The key is over there on the window sill. If you didn't stop for lunch, there's ham and cheese and potato salad in the refrigerator. And now I've got to run. I'll take you out for dinner this evening, and we'll have a nice long chat."

After I'd heard the apartment door close behind her, I still stood there in the little hall, staring with a strange reluctance at that chest. As Mrs. Halliday had said, my mother had stored away in that chest everything that was important to her—official documents, cherished letters and photographs, the gown which she'd worn at her wedding, and which had been altered for me to wear when I married Bill— How utterly defenseless are the dead, I thought. There might be things in that chest that my mother had never intended for even me to see.

It was almost as much my reluctance to go through that chest as my hunger which made me walk down the hall to the kitchen. There I brewed coffee and made a ham sandwich. At last, my footsteps echoing hollowly along the uncarpeted hall, I returned to that bedroom. The light coming through the uncurtained windows was a deeper gray now, and rain struck more sharply at the panes.

Kneeling, I unlocked the chest. I lifted out the tray, with its burden of photograph albums and small cardboard boxes and packets of letters, and placed it on the floor. Then I went through the garments in the lower part of the chest. In a plastic bag that gave off an odor of mothballs was the white satin wedding gown—princess style, with a bodice encrusted with seed pearls—which both my mother and I had worn, and which Nicole might choose to wear someday. I laid it on the cot. Later I'd place it in my almost empty suitcase. I looked through the other garments, two cashmere sweaters, a long evening skirt of plaid wool, an embroidered black wool evening coat, several satin nightgowns, and a paisley shawl. The shawl, I knew, had belonged to my grandmother. I placed it on the cot beside the wedding dress. The rest of the clothing, I decided, along with the chest itself, would go to the Lighthouse for the Blind.

I returned my attention to the contents of the tray. The photograph album had been long familiar to me. As a little girl I'd loved looking at its pictures of my grandfather, and of my mother and her sister as children and young girls. I placed it on the cot. Here was a long jeweler's box, containing the cultured pearls my father had given my mother. That, too, went with the things I intended to keep. Here was a large manila envelope, containing a copy of her will and other documents. Without going through them, I placed them on top of the album. I picked up a thick, ribbon-tied packet of my own letters, dating back to ones I'd sent her from a children's camp in the Poconos when I was eight years old. I'd had no idea she'd saved all my letters. Throat tightening, I placed them on the cot.

Here was a business-sized manila envelope, with no writing whatsoever on it. I opened it, and found another envelope, addressed to Miss Caroline Jessup, at a number on East Twenty-seventh Street, New York City. The ink had faded to brown. The postmark read: "Neptague, N.Y. Oct. 15, 1940."

I stared down at it through the gray light, knowing that it must be Loren Hauklid's last and only letter to the girl my mother once had been—that girl who'd been turned out of her childhood home to make her lonely way in New York. Should I read it? Would she want me to?

As clearly as if she'd been in the room, I recalled her voice saying, "It was a beautiful letter, Cathy, and so—honest." No, she wouldn't mind my reading it.

Taking the single sheet of paper from the envelope, I glanced at the signature, "Loren." Then I read:

> Dearest Caroline,
>
> What can I say to you? That I've been going through hell since you left? But then, so must you have been.
>
> I could see in your face that day your father called the three of us together that you wondered why I didn't protest his exiling you. It was because I knew, my lovely and generous girl, that one of us had to leave here. And it couldn't be me. Marian needs me, and our poor little boy, and your father needs me, too, although nothing on earth could induce him to admit it. I do have hopes of persuading him to change that unjust will. Not for my sake. I'll always be able to make a decent living from the land for my wife and my child, either here or somewhere else. But it's terrible that you should be deprived of all that's rightfully yours.
>
> I've just looked back at the last paragraph and read, "my wife and my child." You see, that's it, Caroline. I

love you. But in a different and deeper way I love Marian —yes, in spite of her bitterness—and the poor little child created by our love. Can you understand that, darling? Can you forgive me? Probably not, considering that in my need I took such advantage of your compassion and tenderness. But try.

There's nothing more to say except that all my life long I'll wish you every good thing. I'll wish you a husband worthy of you. I'll wish you normal and beautiful children. I'll wish you happiness.

Loren

Only half aware of what I was doing, I replaced the letter in its envelope and laid it on the cot. How sad, how terribly sad, to realize that the years could change people that much. In the letter he'd said that he'd always be able to make a decent living from the land for his wife and child. And yet the once-productive acres lay unused, and his wife darned pillow slips, and bartered eggs at the Neptague General Store. He'd said he loved Byron and Marian, and the written words had rung true. And yet since I'd been with the Hauklids I'd never known him to bestow a tender look or word on his son. As for my aunt—well, even if I'd never known about the separate bedrooms, and the summerhouse in the woods, and Edna Carson, I'd have recognized the pinched look of a woman who'd once been beloved, but no longer was.

The chest's tray contained one more object, a box that had once held letter paper. Opening it, I found photographs, ones I'd never seen before. After I'd looked at the first three, I understood why. The Loren of decades ago, but still recognizable, was in all of them. Loren sitting cross-legged on grass—the Jessup lawn?—under a blossoming tree, and smiling at the camera. Young Loren on the seat of a tractor in a field of winter wheat, leaning down to speak to a much older man, whom I recognized from photographs in that album on the cot as my grandfather. The third snapshot, probably taken by my Aunt Marian, was of Loren and my mother and my grandfather, seated on a front porch. Behind them rose the white and gleaming façade of the Jessup house as it had been in those days. The fourth picture wasn't a snapshot, but a time-yellowed photograph clipped from a newspaper. It showed the Neptague Volunteer Firemen, standing proudly in uniform in front of a fire engine, with a smiling Loren at one end of the row. Below the photograph, tiny print announced that it had been taken by someone named Harold Casey, of the *Neptague Messenger.* The next photograph was another snapshot. It was out of focus, but still I could discern Loren and the attractive girl my Aunt Marian once had been leaning over the crowded rail of an ocean liner.

I looked at the next photograph—and caught my breath. Loren was in this one. He was in it twice.

I recalled a photograph in the album of my mother's grammar school graduating class. In it a boy my mother had identified as Melvin Schinn, the class clown, appeared twice. As the camera moved slowly down the long line of children, he'd raced from his position at one end of the row and taken a stance at the other end.

But that couldn't have happened in this case. There were only three people, standing in a blossoming meadow—a girl I recognized as my Aunt Marian, and two young Loren Hauklids.

Dazedly, I turned the photograph over. On its back was the developer's stamp, in a foreign language I realized must be Norwegian. Above the stamp and through it and below it was an ink-written message:

Dear Caroline,

No, your eyes aren't playing you tricks. This is me, and Loren, and Loren's Norwegian first cousin, Eric Hauklid. Isn't it amazing? Like those photographs of George the

Fifth and his cousin, Czar Nicholas. Not to keep you in suspense, Loren is the one on my left.

Much love from your Big Sistie,
Marian

Aware of a ringing in my ears, I turned the photograph over and stared at its face. As if to emphasize their similarity, the two young men had taken a clowning pose, each with a profile to the camera, and a hand on Marian's shoulder. They looked as alike as identical twins. Only as I studied the photograph more closely did I see that the man on the girl's right was perhaps half an inch shorter than Loren, and had a thinner mouth—

I picked up the last photograph in the box. Loren, seated on the front porch of the old Jessup house. On his lap was a child about a year old, whom I knew must be Byron. A grave smile on his lips, Loren supported the child's head with his right hand. Although he must have been only about two years older than the young bridegroom of the Norwegian picture, he appeared to have aged much more than that.

Again I turned my attention to that foreign photograph. And as I stared at it, in my mind's eye I saw another face—Byron's, peering at me around the edge of that standing mirror, his gray eyes luminous in the fading light.

"The one in the mirror," he'd said, "shot the other one."

If a child of three or four, particularly a retarded child, saw those two men facing each other, might he not have thought one was the mirrored image of the other?

With an odd, dream-like detachment I stared down at the photograph. What I was thinking just couldn't be. My Aunt Marian wouldn't have been taken in by an impostor.

And yet—

I reviewed the contradictions. The Loren my mother knew had liked farming; the Loren I knew had let oak and juniper and pitch pine spring up where once corn had ripened, and apple trees bent under their load of fruit. Young Loren had written my mother that he loved his wife and son; the Loren I knew seemed to talk to his son as little as possible, and to treat his wife with—no, not hostility, which might have indicated a once-successful marriage turned sour—but with a calm indifference, as if there'd never been love between them, as if she'd always been to him no more than a housekeeper. Young Loren had liked people and been liked by them; middle-aged Loren seemed to hate large portions of the human race, so much so that he left to his wife all business contacts with people in the village—

In a flash it came to me that it might be fear rather than hate which had led him to isolate himself. Fear that he'd make some slip—fail to recognize, for instance, someone whom a man who'd been Samuel Jessup's farm manager should have recognized.

But that, I realized—vaguely aware that my lips were dry, my heartbeats rapid—would indicate that Aunt Marian knew the identity of the man she called her husband, and had helped him to conceal it. Among other ways, she'd concealed it by keeping her own sister away from the house in which they'd both been born.

And then another flash of memory made me certain she knew his identity. That first night at the Hauklids', I'd told them of Byron's disquieting remark about "the one in the mirror." Pale with terror, she'd stared at her son, that pitiable, thirty-two-year-old child who perhaps had given Eric Hauklid away—

Because it was Eric Hauklid, impostor and almost surely murderer, in that isolated farmhouse.

A dizziness assailed me. I fought it off. Getting to my

feet, I turned toward the hall, intending to hurry toward the phone I'd seen on the floor in the bare living room. Then I checked myself. It would be worse than useless to telephone the Neptague police. Even if I could persuade them to go out to the old Jessup place, which was by no means certain, they wouldn't get inside the house, not without a search warrant, nor would they arrest Eric Hauklid. How could they, with no evidence except my description of an old photograph? All a visit from the police would do would be to alarm and enrage him.

Going out into the hall, I carried my suitcase back into the bedroom, opened it, and swept into it everything I'd laid on the cot except the Norwegian photograph. That I thrust into my handbag. Dimly I was aware that the rain was pounding against the windows now, and that the sycamores outside writhed in the wind. No matter. I'd get back there tonight somehow.

I scribbled a note for Mrs. Halliday—"Sorry, have been called back to Long Island. Please send chest and contents to Lighthouse"—and left it on the cot. Picking up my suitcase, I ran from that empty apartment.

13

Despite my feverish anxiety to get back to the Hauklid house, I had to keep my speed under thirty, even on the well-drained Pennsylvania highways. Rain fell so fast that my windshield wipers couldn't keep the glass clear, and every now and then a gust of wind, like the impact of a giant fist, made my little car rock. But it wasn't until I turned onto the New Jersey Turnpike, where the amber bad-weather warnings glowed through that abnormally early dark, that I learned there might be even worse ahead. The car radio, which I'd kept tuned to an all-news station, told me that the hurricane seemed certain to pass closer to the coast than had been expected earlier, bringing rain and sixty-miles-an-hour winds, with occasional stronger gusts, to New York and parts of Long Island. Already storm-related accidents had blocked some traffic routes, including the one across the Verrazano Bridge. Motorists planning to cross the bridge were advised to use the tunnels instead.

At the entrance to the tunnel running under the Hudson River, I had to wait in line with hundreds of other rush-hour motorists. Until then, driving through the rainy murk had mercifully absorbed all of my attention. But now that I sat idle, thoughts of Nicole brought out cold sweat on my face and the palms of my hands. Nicole, alone there in that wind-and rain-assailed house with a man who'd killed, and a woman who'd concealed the murder of her own husband—

With a desperate effort, I wrenched my thoughts from Nicole and turned them to my aunt. Why had she covered up for Eric Hauklid all these years? Not out of willingness to do so, I was certain. It must have been fear that held her silent. Again I recalled my first night at the Hauklid house, and the terror I'd seen in my aunt's face as she stared at her TV-watching son. The hold of that man over her obviously was connected with her love of Byron, and her fear for him.

But even so, why had she submitted? Eric Hauklid must have usurped his cousin's place many years ago, at least as early as 1943. It was in that year that my mother had married, and had written to her sister about bringing her bridegroom to the old Jessup house for a visit—only to be rebuffed with some vague excuse about such a visit being inadvisable "under the circumstances." In all the years since then, surely, she and Byron should have been able to slip away. And once beyond Eric Hauklid's reach, she could have called the police.

No, it must be something else that had held her—helpless, frightened, scrimping, telling her inexpert lies—in that neglected old house. Little wonder she'd tried so hard to keep me from coming there. And little wonder Eric Hauklid had tried to frighten me away by firing that bullet through my windshield. Because I was sure, now, that he was the one who'd fired it.

It was my turn to go through the tunnel. When I emerged from its gleaming walls and its air smelling of exhaust fumes, I found the rainy and wind-swept streets of

Manhattan almost empty of pedestrians. Driving across town, I entered the Midtown Tunnel. At its end, a little of the tension went out of me. Even though I still had about a hundred miles to drive, I at least was on Long Island.

A century later—after I'd nearly stalled in a flooded underpass on the Long Island Parkway, after a slickered policeman in Riverhead had told me how to bypass high tension wires lying in the middle of the highway, after I'd waited near Southampton, with other motorists, while a highway repair crew hauled a fallen tree out of the road—after all that, I finally found myself moving along the highway that bordered my grandfather's land. My headlights shone on a poster affixed to a telephone pole. The bright colors had been blurred by the pounding rain, but I could make out the words, "Haley Brothers Circus." No doubt, I thought fleetingly, the circus had postponed its opening until tomorrow night.

A few minutes later I turned onto the private road. Rain, slashing down through my headlights' path, shone like a curtain of long silver needles, many layers deep. Sodden branchlets of oak and maple whipped out to plaster themselves briefly against the windshield. I forced myself to slow to ten miles an hour. At any greater speed, I might ram into the trunk of a fallen tree before I even saw it. Thank God, I thought, for those layers and layers of dead leaves in the ruts. Perhaps they'd enable me to reach the house without getting mired down. If not, I'd walk the rest of the way.

I turned a curve. Only a few yards ahead was the break in the trees that marked the little graveyard. Starting past it, I glanced at the white-railed enclosure.

A light in there. A lantern, on the ground. I saw a dark figure rush to the lantern, bend over to extinguish it—

In my startled fear, I lifted my foot from the accelerator. The little car bucked. It rolled on, carrying me a few feet past the graveyard. Then the engine coughed and died. With frantic, fumbling fingers I turned on the ignition. The only response was an empty whine.

A flashlight's beam bathed the car. To my dazzled eyes, the person behind the flashlight was only a dark shape. The beam vanished. Then someone wearing a wet black slicker jerked the door open and slid onto the seat beside me.

"Catherine!" Philip said. "I thought you were in Philadelphia."

For a moment, in my tremulous relief, all I could do was cling to the steering wheel with both hands. Then I asked, in a voice that shook, "What were you *doing?*"

After several seconds he said, "I was putting the sod back on a grave, Jethro Jessup's grave. You see, I opened it tonight."

My fear rushed back. Shrinking from him, I looked at his face, thin and tense in the headlights' refracted glow. "Why—?"

"It was another man's grave, too. Your uncle's. I'm sure his is the second body in the grave. For a lot of reasons, I think Loren Hauklid was buried there sometime in the summer of nineteen forty-two."

When I didn't speak, he said, "I'm sorry you had to learn it like this. I thought you were a couple of hundred miles away. That's why I chose tonight to do this. That and the storm, of course."

I said, with a wild surge of hope, "You are some kind of policeman, aren't you?"

"No. And I haven't wanted to go to the police until I had all the evidence I need. I haven't wanted to—alert him by having some agent coming around to question him." He put his hands on my shoulders. "Catherine, you've got to keep quiet about this. He mustn't have a chance to get away." Bitterness came into his voice. "He was directly responsible for at least one other death, and indirectly for God knows how many."

I reached for the ignition key. Again that empty whine. I said desperately, "I've got to get to Nicole—"

Getting out, he went around to the other side of the car. I slid over. Sitting behind the wheel, he turned on the ignition, fed gas cautiously with his foot. The engine caught. As he drove ahead at the same slow speed I'd forced upon myself, I leaned back in the corner of the seat, eyes closed, heart pounding.

When I could speak, I asked, "How did you know Loren Hauklid was buried there?"

"I didn't, for sure. I thought he was probably buried on Hauklid property, but it might have been in the swamp, or almost anyplace."

"Have—have you been looking in the swamp?"

"No. How could I? It's so close to the house that the Dobermans would have been sure ro raise hell. Besides, when I first came on the Hauklid property—that was last June—it occurred to me that one of the safest places to hide a body would be a grave already in existence."

"But why Jethro Jessup's—?"

"Two reasons. I knew Loren Hauklid must have been so tall that only that grave was long enough. And I saw that the headstone had been reset. Later headstones have sunk until the last line of engraving is barely visible. But this headstone, the oldest in the plot, had sunk no lower than the newest one."

The newest one. My grandfather's.

"Besides, for several inches above the ground that headstone was badly discolored, as if from a hundred years of being buried in the earth. So I waited for a night like this, a night when I could be almost sure there'd be no one else moving around in these woods—" He broke off, and then said, "Look here, I've just realized that you don't seem particularly surprised by the idea of Loren Hauklid being dead." His voice sharpened. "Why not?"

I told him. I don't know what words I used, but they must have been coherent enough, because he didn't interrupt with questions. When I'd finished, he asked, "Where's that photograph?"

"In my handbag."

He took his right hand from the wheel and extended it toward me. "Give it to me." When I hesitated, he repeated, "Give it to me! Don't you realize it's dangerous for you to have it? If he saw it, or perhaps even if one of those other two saw it—"

I gave him the picture. Unfastening the top button of his slicker, he thrust the photograph inside. I said, "If you're not the police, then why—?"

"Eric Hauklid caused my father's death."

He went on talking, knuckles white as he gripped the steering wheel, dark face bitter in the wavering light that came through the streaming windshield. He'd been born in Norway, he told me, three years before the outbreak of the Second World War. His Lutheran minister father had been almost as interested in helping educate young members of his parish as in saving their souls. During the nineteen-thirties he spent all of a legacy he'd received, plus sums raised from his wealthier parishioners, to provide scholarships for secondary students at schools both in Norway and abroad. Among the teen-agers he helped was Eric Hauklid, the eldest offspring of a not very prosperous farmer.

"My mother says that Eric Hauklid was my father's favorite, perhaps because he had such a talent for languages. My father had a theory that through knowing languages other than their own, the people of various countries could draw closer together, and learn to live in peace. Anyway, during the early thirties he sent Eric to a school in this country—my mother thinks it was in Connecticut—for three years, and then to a school in Austria for one year. It must have been there that he became a Nazi, because he came home in nineteen thirty-four spouting ideas about Nordic supremacy. I knew nothing of that, of course. I wasn't born until two years later."

After the Germans invaded Norway in 1940, Philip's father, like many Norwegians, joined the Underground Resistance. Eric Hauklid, who was twenty-four by that time, became an open collaborator with the Germans. "But he went on coming to the parish house, and my father went on admitting him to his study. Because my father had been so fond of him, my mother thinks, he couldn't believe there was no way of turning Hauklid back toward decency. And certainly my father never thought that someone upon whom he'd lavished concern and affection, as well as money, would ever betray him personally."

Eric Hauklid had betrayed him, though. "On one of his visits to the parish house he found something that identified my father as a Resistance member. My mother thinks it must have been a coded message from the local Resistance leader. Anyway, Eric took it to the German Commandant in the district, and soldiers came and took my father, and drove him to the Town Hall, and shot him to death in the courtyard there."

I said, "Oh, Philip! How awful!"

And that was the man under whose roof I'd left my little girl. I ached to urge Philip to drive faster, but I knew how foolishly dangerous that would be. Besides, we'd be there in a few minutes.

"I was only five then," Philip was saying. "In nineteen forty-two, when I was six, Eric Hauklid disappeared from our village. No one seemed to know where he'd gone. But already I'd made up my mind that someday I'd try to find him."

He braked the car to a stop. I cried, "Why are you stopping?"

"Because if I drive any closer, he might hear the car stop, and the door slam, and then the car move on again. He'd wonder who you were letting off in the woods on a night like this."

Again his hands gripped my shoulders. In the watery light coming through the windshield, his face was stern. "Don't talk to anyone about this, not until I come to get you and Nicole out of there. That might be as soon as day after tomorrow, perhaps even sooner. You'll be perfectly safe, as long as he doesn't know he's been found out. I think that now I can get the authorities to move in on him—fast. But if you behave in a way that arouses his suspicion—"

"I won't."

"If you need me, you can call me at the university during the day, and at the Faculty Club at night."

He gave me the Faculty Club number, and had me repeat it three times. "Write it down as soon as you can. It isn't in the phone book yet."

He kissed me, hard, and then got out of the car. For a moment after I started inching the car forward, I could see him in the rear-view mirror, trudging back along the road. Then rain and darkness swallowed him up.

It seemed a strange coincidence, I reflected fleetingly, that Philip should have taken a teaching job at a college only ten miles from where Eric Hauklid led his strange, isolated existence. And then I realized it wasn't a coincidence at all.

A girl had broken off with him, Philip had told me, because he'd chosen to leave a job with an old, prestigious university for a no-doubt lower paying one with an institution only a few years old. "I'd spent several weeks out here the previous summer," he'd said, "and I'd liked what I'd seen of the Hamptons."

He also must have seen the Hauklid name—an uncommon name indeed—on no-trespassing signs strung out for nearly a mile along the highway.

Probably he'd asked a few seemingly casual questions of local people, and learned that in the early nineteen-forties an abrupt change had come over Loren Hauklid. "Turned into a regular hermit," I could imagine some of the older people saying. "Even stopped farming. And the funny thing is, when he first came here to work for Old Man Jessup, he was real popular and outgoing. Why, the Volunteer Firemen took him in right away, and they don't often do that."

According to Steve Connery, Philip Owen had often come into the *Messenger* office to look through the back files. Undoubtedly he'd run across that group photograph of the Volunteer Fire Department—and seen a face almost identical with that of his father's betrayer smiling up at him.

Had that been sufficient? Or had there been something else to convince him that the man who called himself Loren Hauklid had once been a strutting young Quisling in a Norwegian village?

That bent little finger on his left hand.

Steve Connery must have noticed it, the day he came to the old Jessup place to assail Hauklid bitterly over his brother-in-law's death. And Philip Owen must have remembered that finger. A deformity of that sort would stick in a child's mind. During one of his visits to the *Messenger* office, Philip must have asked questions about the Loren Hauklid whose name was strung out all along the highway, until he elicited that last, clinching bit of information about the deformed finger.

"He fell from a horse when he was a child, and the finger was reset badly," my aunt had told me. Undoubtedly that was the case. But it was the Norwegian Hauklid, not the American one, who'd fallen. No wonder my aunt had turned pale almost the instant she'd spoken. She'd feared that I might wonder why my mother had never mentioned that bent finger to me.

My aunt. Why had she given shelter to her husband's murderer? And Eric Hauklid himself. Why had he come here in the first place, and why had he endured a bleak, impoverished existence for so many years? Since he'd been clever enough to devise some way of frightening my aunt into docility, surely he should have been able to devise means of living safely in more pleasant surroundings.

But none of that mattered right now, I thought, as I drove into the farmyard. All that mattered was getting to Nicole, and not letting her out of my sight until Philip came to take us both away from here.

14

As long as Eric Hauklid believed himself safe, Philip had said, Nicole and I would be safe. His words had lessened my anxiety at the time. But now, as I turned off the ignition, my fear flooded back. Hauling my suitcase from the rear seat to the front, I carried it out into the storm-lashed dark, and slammed that balky door.

I'd thought that the storm, although slackening now, might cover that slamming sound. But no. It had reached the Dobermans' ears, and now they were adding their clamor to the drum of rain and the seethe of wind through the trees.

Despite the darkness and the curtain of rain, I could make out the dim bulk of the house. Weak light was filtering through the window of the room the Hauklids had assigned to Nicole and me. From its faintness and its color, I guessed that it was an oil lamp, probably shining from the hall through the open door of that upstairs room. As I ran across the muddy yard, I recalled Steve Connery saying that even moderate storms often knocked out light and power on eastern Long Island. Using my key, I stepped into the lower hall, and then turned to close the door.

Someone said, in a harsh whisper, "Catherine!"

I whirled around. In an old red bathrobe, my aunt stood on the stair landing. Lamplight shining from somewhere at her left showed me the strained pallor of her face.

Fear twisted my stomach. As I raced up the stairs, I called, "Is Nicole—?"

"Sh-h-h! She's fine." When I reached the landing, my aunt caught my arm. "Why are you back? What happened?"

Appalled, I stared at her strained face. In my anxiety to get to my child, I hadn't thought to prepare any explanation for my early return. I said feebly, "I'd done everything I needed to down there, so I decided to come back."

"Through this storm?" Her frightened face took on a pleading look. "Don't lie to me, Catherine; don't lie to me. You don't know how important—"

"Please, Aunt Marian!" I whispered. "Let go of me. I want to see Nicole."

She released me, and I hurried down the hall. Yes, there was the lamp, on a table a few feet beyond the partially opened door of our room.

I hurried in. Light from the hall showed me Nicole asleep in her little bed, her chest rising and falling gently. Neil was curled up behind her head on the pillow. Setting down my suitcase, I moved the kitten to the foot of the bed. Then I turned and went past the big double bed, its sheet and blanket thrown back, where my aunt had been lying.

She stood out in the hall, near the table where the oil lamp burned. Here in the stronger light I could see that fear had dilated her pupils, so that her normally light blue eyes looked dark. "You see," she said, "she's all right. Now tell me. You found something among your mother's things, didn't you? I was afraid you might, and yet I couldn't think of any way of stopping you—"

"Aunt Marian—"

"Don't try to lie to me. The truth's in your face. Anyway, I knew it the instant I heard your car door slam. Unless she was desperate, only a crazy person would drive over two hundred miles on a night like this, and you're not crazy."

Torn with indecision, I stared at her. She'd crossed her thin arms across her chest to still the trembling of her body. Pity for her mingled with my anxiety for Nicole and myself.

"Tell no one," Philip had said. But he hadn't foreseen my aunt's reaction to my early return, any more than I had. If I left her in this distracted state, surely that cold-eyed man who posed as her husband would notice, and instantly conclude that something had gone wrong.

She turned her head, looking down the black corridor that led through the main body of the house to the other wing. Then her pleading eyes returned to my face.

"He won't know," she said. Bitterness crept into her voice. "He's a sound sleeper. I'm the one who's lain awake nights for years and years. Probably he didn't even hear you slam the car door. His room's over near the end of the south wing, and what with the wind and the rain—"

"But the dogs barked."

"They've barked several times since around seven tonight, when it started to get bad out here. Storms make them restless." Her voice became feverishly urgent. "He won't have to know you drove through the storm. It's going to clear here soon. Around midnight, the radio said. It must have cleared already in Philadelphia. We'll say you didn't get home until around three in the morning. You had some sort of argument with Mrs. Halliday, and you couldn't stay there. You saw the weather was clearing, so you drove home."

I looked at her, still undecided. "And you won't tell him anything I—"

"Oh, God! Oh, God, no!" Again she grasped my arm. "Tell me!"

I'd trust her. She'd given me no reason not to, so far. She'd promised to care for Nicole as if she were her own, and she had. Besides, she'd already guessed that somehow I'd learned the truth.

"I found a photograph. A picture of you and your husband and his cousin. You'd mailed it from Norway to my mother, with a note on the back."

I'd feared she might faint. In fact, I'd caught hold of her arms in the old bathrobe to break her fall. But instead both her face and her voice grew calmer. Perhaps knowing beyond a doubt that I shared her secret lightened the burden of it, if only a little.

"And that was enough to make you decide—"

"No, there were other things. He's so different from the Loren Hauklid my mother described to me."

"Yes, very different." Her voice was quiet, almost dull, but I caught a glimpse of a terrible grief behind those words.

"And then there's that twisted finger, the one you said he'd broken in childhood. My mother never mentioned that. And in that photograph your husband had his right hand on your shoulder and his left hand at his side. It had no bent finger."

I thought, "Stop talking about that picture!" She might ask to see it. And I couldn't tell her I'd given it to Philip. I mustn't even mention Philip.

Her face went suddenly rigid. "Have you called the police?"

"No."

"Oh, thank God, thank God."

She did sway then. I grasped her arms. "I'm all right," she said. "We'll go downstairs. I'll tell you everything. And then you'll see why you mustn't tell the police, ever."

"Not downstairs. I want to stay near Nicole."

"All right." Taking the oil lamp from the table, she moved to the room opposite Nicole's and mine. When she opened the door, a musty smell came out. Leaving Nicole's door partly open, I followed her across the hall and into the room.

Obviously it was used for storage. The lamp's warm glow fell upon a horsehair sofa with sagging springs, three straight chairs with broken rush seats, and several barrels. Placing a lamp on one of the barrels, she started to close the door.

"Oh, please! I want to be able to see Nicole's door."

She nodded. Turning back, she took a faded old sofa pillow of flowered cretonne from atop a barrel and placed it over the broken seat of one of the chairs. Then she sank onto the corner of the sofa where the springs still held.

15

For a moment after I'd sat down on the chair, my aunt remained silent. Then she said, "Maybe you don't know about it, since it happened before you were born. But one night in June of nineteen forty-two, a Nazi submarine landed four saboteurs on a beach about two miles from here. The men came ashore in a rubber boat, bringing a case of explosives with them."

I stared at her incredulously. "Are you trying to say—? But that can't be! I learned a little about that in school. And Steve Connery has a book about that case in his office. I read most of it. There were eight saboteurs in all. The submarine landed four of them out here, and the other four in Florida. Within a week, all eight had been rounded up. Six of them were executed. The other two were imprisoned for a while, and then sent back to Germany after the war. Eric Hauklid couldn't possibly have been—"

"Eric Hauklid," she said quietly, "had been landed twenty-four hours before the others, by another submarine. But I'd better start at the beginning. I mean, with our honeymoon, Loren's and mine." Her voice broke.

"Oh, Catherine! Sometimes I can't believe I was ever that young and happy. But I was."

Unable to look at her pain, I averted my eyes. After a moment she went on, more quietly, "Father had given us that wedding trip to Norway, so that we could see the place where Loren's parents had been born, and where his aunt and uncle and their family still lived."

They'd liked Loren's Uncle Sven and Aunt Karen, and their three younger children. The eldest one, about a year older than Loren, had been a different story. "Some clergyman had sent Eric to school in Germany, or maybe Austria, I forget which, and he'd come back filled with wild ideas. There was going to be another world war soon, he said—this was in nineteen thirty-seven—and Germany was sure to win because this time America would be on Germany's side. America was full of what he called Nordics, people of English and German and Scandinavian descent, and they'd realize that Hitler's cause was their cause. Not even the international bankers, whoever he meant by that, would be able to drag America into a war against Nazi Germany.

"Loren and I were appalled and disgusted, but we tried not to show it. We didn't want to upset Uncle Sven and Aunt Karen. Besides, we were young and terribly in love, and we didn't want arguments shadowing our happiness." Her mouth twisted. "Perhaps if we had argued with him, if we'd showed him that we were neither docile nor stupid—"

She went on, telling of their return to the old Jessup house, and of Byron's birth, and of their pride in their son gradually turning to anxiety and then to sorrow. With embarrassed color staining her cheekbones—my face, too, felt warm—she hurried over that tumultuous summer when Loren, in his lonely sense of rejection, had turned briefly to my mother. She spoke of my mother's departure from this house, and of my grandfather's death only a few months later.

"I think that was what drew Loren and me together again. We'd both loved him so. We'd felt that he'd been cruel and unjust in sending Caroline away, and in drawing up that new will, but that didn't keep us from loving him, or from grieving when we lost him. Within a few months after his death, we were closer than we'd ever been. And we were happy, not just because of each other, but because of Byron. It hurt terribly to know his mind would never grow up. But he was such a good, cheerful little boy that we took joy in him anyway."

I said, from a tight throat, "I'm glad you had some good years."

"We did. In fact, soon after Byron's fourth birthday, we began to discuss whether or not we'd risk having another child."

But they didn't have a chance to come to a final decision on that, because one June evening the doorbell rang. Eric Hauklid, dressed in a khaki work shirt and trousers, and carrying a small duffel bag by its handle, stood on the porch.

"We couldn't believe our eyes. America was at war with Nazi Germany. Norway had been occupied by the Germans for more than two years, and so of course there was no ship traffic between Norway and the United States. And yet here stood Loren's Norwegian cousin.

"He went with us into the living room, and sat down, and told us this preposterous story. He'd broken with the Nazis, he said. In fact, they'd been hunting him down to kill him. Friends had smuggled him across the border to Sweden, where he'd bribed his way aboard an America-bound freighter. Two sailors in a lifeboat had rowed him ashore at Montauk Point. From there he'd hitched rides. The last motorist had known where our place was, and had let him off at our private road.

"We didn't believe it, of course. In the first place, he'd been a Nazi when Norway was a country where most people openly loathed Nazis. Why should he have broken with them, now that they were in power? Besides, it seemed most unlikely that a ship's captain from a neutral country would land an immigrant illegally. I think only someone like him would have expected to be believed."

I nodded, picturing the three of them in that living room, a room that must have been far more cheerful in those days. Yes, I thought, only a totalitarian, with a totalitarian's contempt for most of the human race, would have expected that they would believe him.

"Loren asked why he hadn't stayed in Sweden. He said he was afraid to, that someone he recognized as an enemy had been following him on a Stockholm street. Then Loren said he was sorry, but Eric would have to report himself as an illegal immigrant."

Their Norwegian cousin had grown very excited at that. If he reported himself, he'd be killed. Everyone knew that America was full of Nazi sympathizers, many of them in touch with Nazis abroad.

No, Loren told him firmly, America was far from being filled with Nazi sympathizers. And he'd be perfectly safe. The worst that could happen to him would be internment until after the war.

"He just sat there quietly for a while after that. Then he asked us to give him a chance to rest for a day. He felt very tired, and he'd been seasick most of the time on the freighter. If we gave him until day after tomorrow, he'd report himself to the Immigration people.

"We gave in. After all, there was just a chance that his story might be true. Stranger things than that have happened in wartime. Besides, we were a little afraid of him. We thought he might have a gun in that duffel bag, and there was a child in the house."

That night they'd taken Byron into their room to sleep, and had locked their bedroom door. Saying at breakfast that he still felt tired, Eric Hauklid spent most of the next day in the room they'd assigned to him.

Several times that day, Loren and Marian discussed calling the Immigration Department. At last they decided to keep their word to him. After all, he was a cousin. But if Eric didn't report the next day, Loren himself would notify the authorities.

"At dinner that night," my aunt went on, "Eric seemed calm, even cheerful. He'd decided we were right, he told us. It was only the state of his nerves that had made him feel that even in America he'd be in danger. And internment wouldn't be so bad. At least he'd still be alive at the end of the war.

"After dinner he listened to a couple of radio programs with us. Then, even though a thick fog had rolled in, one of the worst I've ever seen, he said he felt restless and needed a walk. He went up to his room, came down wearing a canvas jacket, and went out."

He hadn't come back for nearly three hours. At first the Hauklids thought he might have gotten lost in the fog. Then they began to fear he'd slipped away and taken a train to New York. "The truth was, of course," my Aunt Marian said, "that he'd gone down to the beach to meet those four saboteurs. Not that they knew he was coming, or even that such a person as he was in this country. After —after Loren was dead, Eric boasted to me that he was the only one of the nine men landed by German submarines who had the confidence of the Nazi Party."

She went on, explaining that the rivalry among the various German intelligence agencies of the time had been even sharper than the present-day rivalry of the FBI, CIA, NSA, and other such agencies in this country. The Nazi Party's own intelligence department had felt that the saboteurs, trained by members of Abwehr, the regular German army's intelligence department, were a bunch of incompetents, which, of course, they turned out to be. And so, without even notifying Abwehr, Nazi Intelligence had sent Eric ahead of the others. He was to meet the saboteurs after they landed, show them orders signed by Heinrich Himmler, the chief of the Gestapo, and take charge of the group's operations in this country.

"He was standing there in the fog, beside a sand dune, ready to step forward when— But if you've read about that night, you know what happened."

I nodded, imagining the alarm Eric Hauklid must have felt as, invisible in the thick fog, he heard those would-be saboteurs calling out to each other on a Long Island beach—in German! His alarm must have turned to fury when he heard one of the group threaten the patrolling coast guardsman he'd blundered into, and then offer him money to keep silent. And when Eric Hauklid saw the German commit that folly of follies—shine a flashlight on his own face—his rage and despair must have been boundless.

"When he finally walked back into the house," my aunt said, "we'd already made up our minds to report him. His face was awful—dead-white, with a vein throbbing in one temple—and he was swearing in Norwegian. Loren had taught me a little Norwegian. I caught the word 'fool,' and something I think was 'traitor.'

"Loren interrupted him to ask just when in the morning he planned to turn himself in. Eric said, in English, 'I'm not going to. Part of my work here is ruined. Those fools—or maybe at least one of them is a traitor—will be picked up in no time at all.'

"Loren asked him what the hell he was talking about. Eric said, 'You'll see. I can still be useful here. My superiors and I worked out alternative plans in case those fools did something like this. Now I'll put those plans into effect.'

"Loren said, 'I still don't know what you're talking about. But if you're not going to report yourself to Immigration, I'm going to report you, and right now.'

He'd gotten up then, and moved toward the hall. Drawing a gun from inside his coat, his cousin had followed him.

Aunt Marian said, her voice low and breathy now, "I don't remember moving from my chair, but I must have, because all of a sudden I was standing in the doorway between the living room and the hall. I saw Loren walking toward the phone. Eric called, 'Loren!' and when Loren turned around, he—shot him. Not just once. Perhaps four or five times while—while Loren was going down. I saw—I saw blood all over the hall runner. Then I heard a whimpering noise. Byron was crouched on the stairs, looking down from between the spokes of the banister."

She'd made me see it, too. Her child looking down at her husband, lying in his own blood on the hall runner—that Aubusson runner which his murderer must later have destroyed.

She was lying back in the corner of the horsehair sofa now, eyes closed. Her white, suffering face made me want to say, "Don't talk about it any more, not now!" But I couldn't say that. If I was to help her, there were things I had to know.

I said, "And—after that, Aunt Marian?"

She opened her eyes. "I don't know. I mean, I blacked out then. When I came to, I was on the floor of that sewing room downstairs. Its door was locked. I could hear Byron crying somewhere upstairs. I kept pounding on the door and shouting. Finally I heard a car drive in. It was our car. I knew he must have used it to take Loren somewhere—"

She broke off for a moment, and then went on speaking. "I heard him come into the living room, and I screamed at him, but he ignored me for a long, long time, maybe half an hour. When he finally unlocked the door, he had a gun in his hand. He made me go over to the desk, and he held the gun at my head while I copied this statement he'd written out."

"Statement?"

"A—a confession. It said that I'd helped him murder my husband. It said that in Norway he'd—converted me to his political views, and that we'd fallen in love." I saw her give a slight shudder. "It said a lot of things. And at the end it said that I was giving this statement to him, and he was giving a similar one to me, in case either of us was ever tempted to betray the other. He gave me no such statement, of course. He just took the one I'd copied out. I don't know where it is, but I'm sure he still has it."

I stared at her in astonishment and pity. "Is *that* the hold he's had over you? Don't you realize that if you'd gone to the police, they'd have believed you, not that piece of paper?"

"Perhaps, if I'd gone right then. But he gave me no chance to. He shut me in an upstairs room, far enough away from the one where he'd put Byron so that I could scarcely hear him crying. He made me drink some of the port wine Loren and I had kept on the dining room sideboard. Maybe he'd put some of my own sleeping pills in it. Maybe it was some dope he'd brought with him. Anyway, I slept until about noon the next day, and when I woke up, I found he'd tied me to the bed, and gagged me with—one of Loren's neckties."

I asked, sickened, "Do you think that Byron—?"

"Probably Eric had gagged him, too. I didn't hear him crying. After a while Eric came in. He took the gag out of my mouth, and gave me something to eat, and told me that he'd run our car deep into the woods. He'd also put a printed note in a milk bottle on the front porch, saying that we'd gone to Canada for three weeks. Then he put the gag back in my mouth and went out, locking the door.

"I don't know exactly how long I was in that room. Later he told me it was three weeks, and I guess it was about that long. He kept me doped up most of the time, as well as gagged. Once I thought of refusing to eat or drink. But I knew that I'd have to keep up my strength as much as I could, for Byron's sake."

I thought of her lying there, racked with grief in her waking moment for her husband, and with terror for her child. "Did he let you see Byron?"

"He let me hear him. He walked back and forth with Byron outside the door. Byron called him Papa." Her voice was touched with the wonder and disbelief she must have felt that long-ago day. "I guess Eric had persuaded him that the one who'd—lived was his father. In later years Byron never mentioned what he'd seen in the lower hall that night. I thought he'd forgotten it. But I guess he hadn't, not entirely. For one thing, it was after Loren's death that Byron started sleepwalking. Again and again I've found him at the same spot on the stairs where he'd looked down through the banisters that night. And then, there was that thing he said to you about the one in the mirror—"

"Probably he doesn't really remember it. Maybe he only remembers bits of it, when something brings it into his consciousness. You know, the way you won't remember a dream until something that happens the next day brings part of it back to you."

She nodded. "Perhaps."

"Didn't anyone come to the house while you were locked in that room?"

"Yes. The first afternoon I heard a truck drive in. I guess whoever it was read the note in the milk bottle. Anyway, he drove off without ringing the doorbell. Two days later someone else drove in and then out, the same way. For the first few days I heard the phone ring now and then. After that, nothing. I guess word had gotten around that the Hauklids were away on a trip."

She fixed her gaze broodingly on some point on the wall behind me. "I often think of how if he'd come here two months earlier he'd never have gotten away with it. There'd have been farm laborers around. But planting time was long since over—we'd put the land into early potatoes that year—and so when Eric turned up there were only the three of us here."

She stopped speaking. In the silence, I became aware that the wind had died, and the rain slackened to just a gentle tapping against the pane.

In a moment or so she went on, "I realized after a while that he couldn't keep me up there much longer, not unless he wanted to risk showing himself in the village to buy supplies. He'd been bringing me fruits and vegetables I'd canned the summer before, and ham and bacon and tongue that Loren had home-cured. Because it was wartime, the government had urged people to raise and can their own food, and so Loren and I had laid by as much preserved food as we could. Still, I realized supplies must be getting low.

"Finally, one morning after breakfast I didn't go back to sleep again, and so I knew he'd stopped drugging me. Around three o'clock he came into the room and took the gag out of my mouth. He had everything worked out, he said. From now on, he was Loren Hauklid. He'd practiced Loren's signature so that he could duplicate it, if he had to. But he wouldn't have to very often, because I was going to transact all business for the Hauklids. He'd never go into the village at all, if he could possibly help it. Late in the summer I'd arrange to have some other farmer harvest the potatoes, on shares. I was to tell the farmer that my husband was too sick to come into the fields himself. But after that there'd be no more farming. He'd looked through all the financial correspondence in the house, and he knew that income from the trust my father had set up would keep us from starving.

"I told him that people would wonder about his behavior. He said that I was to hint that my husband had suffered something almost like a nervous breakdown. 'People won't question you about that,' he said. 'They'll be too embarrassed. And after a while they'll forget that Loren Hauklid was ever anything but a recluse. Anyway, that's the way it's going to be.' And then he reminded me of that statement I'd copied out."

I leaned forward. "And you let him intimidate you with it? Don't you realize that even then if you'd gone to the police—"

"They wouldn't have arrested me, too? Don't be so sure, Catherine. That was wartime, and public feeling was running high. An enemy agent had lived in my house for three weeks. As for what had happened during those three weeks, it would be my word against his—with that statement in my handwriting backing him up. Oh, if I'd had just myself to think of, I'd have gone to the police the first chance I got, and if I hadn't been able to do that, I—might have killed him. But there was Byron."

I said, "I'm still not sure I see—"

"If I'd gone to jail for treason, or for murder, what would have happened to Byron? Even if the authorities had eventually believed me, the Child Welfare Department might have decided that he'd undergone such a horrible experience in this house, and while under my care, that he'd be better off someplace else. And you know what sort of place that would have been, don't you?"

Appalled understanding held me tongue-tied.

"A normal little boy might have been adopted. But who'd knowingly adopt a child who'd never grow up? He'd have been shut away in an institution." Her voice rose slightly. "That's what will happen now, too, if anyone else hears about this. All I have in the world now is the knowledge that Byron is happy. He has to stay that way, for my sake as well as his own."

I looked down at my hands, clasped tightly in my lap. Was she right? Would she be jailed, and Byron shut away someplace, with overworked attendants who'd feed and care for his adult body, but not that loving and generous young-child heart of his? With despair, I realized that might happen. Whatever her reasons, for many years she'd protected a murderer and an avowed enemy of her country.

But there was nothing I could do about it. Her fate and Byron's—and Eric Hauklid's—were in Philip Owen's hands. And he wouldn't turn aside now from his long-held determination to see Hauklid brought to book.

Her eyes, red-rimmed with fatigue in her white face, pleaded with me. "You won't tell anyone?"

"No, I won't tell."

Technically, it wasn't a lie. I wouldn't tell, because there was no need to now. And yet the sense of my duplicity sickened me. For a moment I was almost overwhelmed by an impulse to warn her that Eric Hauklid's arrest, and possibly her own, was only hours away. But I mustn't do that. In her terror it would be almost certain that she'd suggest to Hauklid that the two of them, with Byron, try to escape. And then I, too, would have been guilty of aiding that monstrous man.

Wearily she stood up. "We both better try to sleep."

"Yes."

We moved out into the hall. As she replaced the lamp on the hall table, I asked, "Won't you need that to get back to the south wing?"

"After a lifetime in this house?" Her smile held no humor at all. "I could find my way blindfolded over every inch of it. Goodnight, Catherine."

I watched her until she disappeared in the blackness beyond the landing. I, too, I decided, could do without the lamp. The tiny flashlight in my purse would enable me to find anything I needed as I prepared for bed, and it would be less disturbing to Nicole. Lifting the lamp's chimney, I blew out the flame and, after a moment's fumbling, fitted the chimney into the little circle of wire prongs that held it upright. Then, in the pitch darkness, I turned toward the door of my room.

A stair creaked under someone's foot.

16

There in the blackness, I stood rigid. Byron, down there on the stairs? Byron, walking in his sleep?

Of course it was Byron, I told my suddenly racing heart. In a moment I'd hear him descending the stairs, or perhaps climbing them.

I heard nothing. That other person must be standing motionless, holding his breath just as I held mine.

Paralysis left me. I slipped inside my room, fastened that pitifully inadequate hook, and stood with my back to the door. A faint luminosity—starlight?—coming through the window showed me the shape of Nicole's body in the little bed. I stared at her, trying to marshal my panic-scattered thoughts.

Eric Hauklid, slipping along that second-floor corridor under cover of the diminishing storm and the sound of our voices, then retreating swiftly partway down the stairs when my aunt said, "We'd both better try to sleep." How much had he heard? Instantly I realized it didn't matter how much or how little he'd heard. Even a sentence or two would have told him that his identity had been revealed.

That is, if he'd really been there.

Old houses creak. Of course they do. Stairs especially. The chances were that neither he nor Byron had been standing there.

Go to bed, I commanded myself. You're exhausted. Sleep.

But of course I didn't. I didn't even undress, except for my shoes. There in the darkness, I spread up the bed my aunt had occupied, and lay down on the coverlet. Then, unable to keep still, I moved to the window. The trees across the clearing stood motionless. Above them the stars shone as serenely as if the storm had never been.

Such utter silence. Perhaps because of the drenching rain that had just passed, even the insect voices were stilled. It was as if this house, and the whole night, had drawn itself together to listen.

As Eric Hauklid had listened.

Quite suddenly, I was sure that he had. I was as sure of it as I was of the feel of the rough-textured carpet beneath my stockinged feet, and the sound of my daughter's quiet breathing.

Aware of a high-pitched ringing in my ears, I turned and looked down at Nicole. Should I gather her up, run down to my car, drive off?

Suddenly roused from sleep, she'd cry out. He'd hear her. For he was still awake, planning what to do. Perhaps he'd stop us even before we got out of the house. And even if I did manage to drive off, he'd follow in his own car. I imagined myself speeding down that narrow, winding road with a terrified child on the seat beside me, and his headlights dazzlingly reflected in my rear-view mirror, and, on a curve, a tree trunk looming up—

Philip. Philip could persuade the police to come quickly, and then he'd come here himself. Slip down to the phone and call him. You don't need any sort of light. You can dial that number by touch.

That number. For a terrible instant I couldn't remember it. Then it leaped into my mind. Crossing the room, I soundlessly lifted the hook, slid into the hall.

I stood rigid, listening. No sound anywhere, except the surge of my own blood in my ears. Still, he might be down there, on the stairs or in the lower hall. But I'd go down to that phone, because I had to.

The faintest glimmer of starshine, coming through the front door's fanlight, showed me that no one stood on the stairs. I crept down them. Trailing one hand along the wall, I moved back through deeper darkness to the phone table. As quietly as I could, I lifted the instrument from its cradle.

No dial tone.

Had he cut the wire? And if so, was he still down here, standing only a few feet away in the utter blackness at the rear of the hall? Stop that, I told myself. He wasn't there. Since the storm had knocked out the electricity, it was only to be expected that phone lines also would be down.

With only the slimmest of hopes, I dialed Operator. The phone remained dead.

It made a faint click as I replaced it. I stood there, hand still on the instrument. I'd have to go for help. But first I'd have to ask my aunt to stay with Nicole. Surely she'd understand that I had to bring the police here. Surely she'd see that all our lives were in danger, now that Hauklid knew she'd betrayed him.

I'd have to go on foot, because I dared not let him hear me starting the car. Once I reached the highway, surely I'd find some traffic moving along it. Someone would pick me up, take me to the police—

Which of those rooms in the south wing was my aunt's?

Byron had said, "Papa's room is next to mine." I'd seen Hauklid standing at the fourth window from the end of the south wing. That meant that Byron's was either the third or the fifth from the end. My aunt, surely, would occupy the room on the other side of her son's room. But would that be the second door from the end, or the sixth? Pray God it was the second. Then, after I'd climbed that staircase at the end of the south wing, I wouldn't have to pass the room where perhaps Eric Hauklid sat silent in the dark, with the door open—

Still groping my way, I turned toward the living room. I was only about a third of the way across it when I collided with a straight chair. I managed to catch it before it went over, but the scraping noise its legs made against the floor was loud enough that my heart gave a painful leap. After that I moved more slowly, hands stretched out before me. On the other side of the room I opened a door. Perhaps sixty feet away, starlight glimmered through a long window. Yes, this was the hall leading along the lower floor of the south wing. Moving slowly close to the wall, lest a creaking floorboard betray me, I followed it to its end, and then turned right into another corridor. A few feet ahead, a newel post and a stair rail gleamed faintly. Still keeping close to the wall, I moved up the staircase one slow and soundless step at a time.

Here it was, the second door on the right. Holding my breath, I turned the knob. The lock gave a faint click, and then the door swung back. Puzzled and dismayed, I stared at dully glimmering porcelain. A bathroom.

Had I miscounted, that morning I'd looked up at the south wing's second floor and seen a man's hand release a window curtain? Had he been standing at the fifth window from the end, rather than the fourth? If so, then the third door along this corridor was probably my aunt's.

Moving soundlessly a few more feet along the hall, I grasped the next doorknob. It, too, turned easily under my hand. The door swung back. Starlight showed me a bureau, a single bed.

The man lying on it sat up.

Unable to move, I stared at him. After a moment he said, "Mama?" Then more loudly, in a voice of a child trembling on the brink of fear, "Is that you, Mama?"

His mother's room, I realized numbly, must be right across the hall. Why hadn't I realized it might be?

In the garage out by the workshed, an engine roared into life. I heard a car back out, drive across the farmyard.

For a moment my mind was empty of everything except surprise. Then the man-child on the bed asked, with a whimper, "Where's Papa going?"

Terror engulfed me. I turned. Dimly conscious of the sound of my running feet, I raced along the corridor, across the stair landing, and into my room.

I knew at once that Nicole was gone. I knew it because I could see the blanket tossed back over the railed bed's foot. Nevertheless, I ran over there and groped with both hands over the sheet, calling her name.

Somewhere near my feet, the kitten mewed.

The sound brought me at least partially to my senses. I thought, "Follow him!" Turning, I groped for my handbag on the bureau top, found it. I plunged down the stairs, jerked open the front door, started out onto the little porch.

Two dark shapes, silent and deadly as arrows, coats faintly gleaming in the starlight, hurtled up the steps toward me. I leapt backward and slammed the door, just as one of the dogs thudded against it. They were both leaping against it now, and I felt the door, imperfectly latched, swing inward an inch or two. With all my strength I leaned against it until it closed. One groping hand found the bolt and pushed it into place.

Dimly I was aware of lamplight streaming down the staircase, and my aunt's frightened voice calling, "Catherine, what is it?"

17

Turning, I stood with my back to the door. Again one of the dogs hurled himself against it. I could feel the wood tremble under the impact. And in my mind's ear I could hear my silent screaming.

An oil lamp in her hand, Aunt Marian came down the stairs. She didn't speak again until she stood so close to me that I could feel the lamp's heat.

"Catherine, what's happening?"

I heard my own voice, mechanical as a doll's. "He's let the dogs loose. I can't go after them."

She shook my arm. "Catherine! Try to—"

"Nicole. He's got Nicole."

Her hand dropped from my arm. She said, in a toneless voice, "Oh, my God." After a moment she added, "So he did wake up when you came home. And he listened—"

We stared at each other. Inside me, the silent screaming went on. Then I heard Byron call, "Mama?"

A dim, pajama-clad figure, he stood on the landing. My aunt turned around. "Byron, put the dogs back in the kennel. No, don't go through this door," she said, as he started down the stairs. "Go down the other stairs and out the side door."

He turned toward the south wing. I said, "Can he—?"

"Yes, the dogs obey him."

They'd stopped thudding against the door now, but I knew they must be out there, waiting. I put my hand on the bolt, ready to pull it back the moment the dogs were gone.

My aunt said, "It's no use. You couldn't catch him." She paused. "What did his note say?"

"Note?"

"He must have left one, telling you what to do."

"Yes," I said. "Yes, of course."

The lamp's glow traveled with me as I ran up the stairs, and so I knew my aunt was following. I went into my room. My hands, groping over the bureau top, found the note even before the lamplight fell upon it.

He'd written it on lined paper, torn from a small, loose-leaf notebook. It said, "The child will be all right as long as you don't tell the police or anyone else. I will phone you at eight tonight with instructions."

Standing beside me, my aunt must have read the note too, because she said, "You must do exactly what he tells you to."

"Yes," I said. "Oh, yes!" Dimly I was aware of Byron's voice. He was out in the farmyard now, calling the dogs. "If I do as he asks, will she be—?"

"She'll be safe. In one way, he's a madman, but only in one way. He kidnaped her to keep you quiet. He knows that if he harmed her in any way, nothing on earth could keep you quiet."

My eyes sought the little traveling clock on the bureau. A little past four. Sixteen hours until eight o'clock tonight. Sixteen eternities.

I said, "But how can I live through sixteen hours?"

"You'll sleep."
"Sleep?" I looked at her wonderingly.
"I'll give you sleeping pills. She placed the lamp on the bureau. "Get undressed."
"No, no! I want to be ready if anything—"
"All right. But lie down." I stared, uncomprehending, as she transferred the pillow from the head of the bed to its foot. Then I understood. That way, I wouldn't be able to see the little railed bed.
"Lie down," she repeated. I obeyed. "I'll leave this lamp here, and take the one out in the hall."
When she'd gone, I stared at the small circle of bright light the lamp cast on the ceiling. This wasn't happening. Very soon now, I'd wake up—
My aunt came in, carrying a glass of water, and I knew it wasn't a dream. She held out her hand. Two small yellow capsules lay on her palm. "Take these."
I remained motionless. "The phone. It's dead."
"I know. It went dead early this evening."
My voice rose. "But then how can he call?"
"It won't be dead by eight tonight. They usually get the phones back in service pretty fast. Now take these."
I did. They stuck in my throat. It wasn't until I'd drunk most of the water that they washed down. I asked, "How long—?"
She took the glass from my hand. "You ought to be asleep in about twenty minutes."
"Talk to me until then."
"Of course." Placing the empty glass on the nightstand, she sat down on the edge of the bed, and then just stared at me. With fleeting detachment I realized that my face must look like hers, paper-white, with shock-dilated pupils, and skin drawn taut over the cheekbones.
I groped desperately for something, anything, to start

her talking. I said, "Do you know a woman named Edna Carson?"

She didn't even ask how I heard of the woman. "Yes. She came here one day eight years ago." Her voice, too, was like mine, flat and mechanical. "That was before she opened her beauty parlor. She was selling cosmetics from door to door then."

She stopped speaking. While I was still searching my mind for some question to start her talking again, she went on, "He usually keeps out of sight when anyone shows up here. He didn't act that way with her. He walked out to her car with her when she left, and I could tell he was making a date with her." She added, still in that expressionless voice, "There's a summerhouse in the woods. They've been meeting there ever since."

"Have there been other women?"

"Oh, yes. In Riverhead, I think. As you know, it's a fairly large town, and about twenty-five miles from here. Before he met Edna Carson he used to go there sometimes, late at night. At least, I imagine that's where he went. Several times I found match books on the floor of the car, with advertising from a Riverhead liquor store on them."

She paused, and then added, "He's never even tried to approach me. That's been the one mercy. I couldn't have stood that."

Think of the life he'd led all these years—the lonely, impoverished, furtive life. Think of that. Think of anything but—

"Why has he stayed here? If he'd left, you'd still have kept silent."

"You mean, because of that statement he made me write out. No, he didn't stay here to keep me quiet. I think that at first he expected, or at least hoped, that someone would get in touch with him here about the landing of more saboteurs. I'm sure that no one ever did. In fact, I read somewhere that during the Second World War there wasn't a single case of German sabotage on American soil. I guess the Germans figured one fiasco was enough—"

Her voice trailed off. I said, "But why did he go on staying here after the war?"

"He's a war criminal, remember, and war criminals are still being prosecuted. If he'd left here—well, even if I'd kept silent about what—what he did to Loren, he might have been recognized as a Norwegian Quisling, and extradited for trial." Again she paused, and then added, "Besides, I think he stays because of something he put in the swamp, and then lost track of."

"Something?"

"I don't know what it is, but it must be something he brought from Norway, something that has to do with the assignment the Nazis gave him. About eighteen months before the war ended, we had a bad storm out here, a northeaster. Water broke through from the bay into the swamp. Whatever he'd put there must have been displaced, because it was after that he started going to the swamp at night. He still goes there, every once in a while. Apparently whatever he's lost is so important to him that he's afraid to look for it in the daytime, when someone might wander in there and see him."

The swamp. Carrying Nicole into the swamp— No, no. Don't think.

I said, "But how can anything he put there be important after all these years?"

"I suppose he thinks it may, someday. You see, that's the way in which he's a madman. He still believes his kind are going to win out, all over the world, or at least over most of it. He talks to me about it, since he has no one else to talk to. Every time some strong man overthrows an elected government—in South America, say, or Greece—he's excited and happy. He's pleased by our racial troubles in this country, too. He's sure that soon we'll turn to some American Hitler."

She stopped speaking. I couldn't think of anything to say. In the silence I could hear the tick of the traveling clock. The clock was a mouse, gnawing with tiny teeth at all those hours between now and eight o'clock tonight.

Again my aunt spoke. "For a while I thought that perhaps he'd taken Loren's body to the swamp. I don't now. I'm almost certain where Loren is buried."

A blessed numbness was creeping over me, blurring the light, and the sound of her voice. "One day in the graveyard I saw that Jethro Jessup's gravestone had been reset. I'm sure Loren's buried there. That's why I've been so afraid of people going into that graveyard. And I suppose others have, beside that college teacher."

Philip. Something about Philip I hadn't taken into consideration. Something dangerous.

The thought slipped away. My eyes closed. I was aware of a blanket being spread over me. And then I sank down into sleep as into black, warm water.

18

When I awoke, cool blue light that could have been either dawn or twilight filled the room. Utterly confused, I stared at the mahogany headboard, dark against the yellow wallpaper with its faded pattern of trailing vines. Why was I lying the wrong way in the bed? Why hadn't I undressed?

Recollection swept through me. That terrible, terrible dream. Of course it had been a dream. I'd look around now, and see Nicole sleeping in the dawn light.

Throwing the blanket aside, I sat up, faced the window. The little bed was no longer there. Knowing what the sight of that empty bed would do to me, my aunt must have wheeled it away while I slept my drugged sleep.

Then it had happened; it had happened. And that was evening light out there, not dawn.

My gaze flew to the traveling clock. Twenty of seven. Thank God. Only a little more than an hour to wait until he phoned. And soon after that, I'd have Nicole back.

Unless something went wrong.

It returned to me then, that thought about Philip

which had slipped away from me, uncompleted. My body turned cold.

Philip intended to send police here.

True, he'd said they probably wouldn't come before Thursday, and this was still Wednesday. But what if he decided to move sooner than that?

"The child will be safe," Eric Hauklid had written, "as long as you don't tell the police or anyone else." Probably he was somewhere nearby, where he could keep track of what went on here at the house. If the police came, he'd think I called them—

I'd have to stop Philip. The police mustn't come here tonight, or tomorrow, or anytime until I had Nicole in my arms. I searched my memory for that phone number, found it. Leaning over, I slipped on my shoes. As I ran down the stairs, I heard the blare of the TV set in the living room, and a rasping sound from the kitchen. My aunt, opening the oven door. Swiftly I moved back along the hall to the phone, dialed.

On the third ring a cheerful masculine voice said, "Faculty Club."

"Is Mr. Owen there? Philip Owen?"

"Phil Owen? He's in the dining room. I'll call him."

By the time I heard Philip's voice, my hand holding the phone was wet with sweat. I said, "Philip, it's Catherine. Is anyone else near enough to hear my voice?"

"No, no one." His tone was sharp now. "And there's no switchboard here. What's happened?"

"Have you told the police about—"

"Not yet. I called a Federal agent in Babylon today. That's the nearest office. Tomorrow I'll see him."

"Don't!" I cried. "Don't do anything, not until after I have her back. If you do, he'll think I'm the one who turned him in—"

"Catherine! Tell me what's happened!"

"He's got Nicole. He heard Aunt Marian telling me about him, and he took Nicole."

"Oh, my God!"

Neither of us spoke for a moment. Then he asked, "Do you have any idea where—?"

"No. He just drove off with her. He left this note, saying that if I called the police—"

"Does he know that I know who he is?"

"No."

"I'll be there in twenty minutes."

"No!" I cried frantically. "He might be somewhere nearby. He'd know. Don't come; don't!"

"Catherine—"

"And I must stop talking now. He said he'd call at eight. But maybe he'll call earlier. And don't phone me. If he finds the line busy, he might decide— Just promise me you won't talk to that agent, or the police, or anyone."

"Of course I promise. But, Catherine—"

"I'm going to hang up. Don't call me and don't come here. Don't, don't!"

I replaced the phone, turned, and found my aunt standing only a few feet away, her face pale and drawn in the fading light. She said, "So someone else knows."

"Yes. Philip Owen."

From the living room came the clatter of hooves, and savage war cries, and the crackle of flames. An Indian raid.

"And he intends to send the police here?"

The police, who might arrest not only Eric Hauklid, but the woman who'd sheltered him. Beneath my terror for Nicole stirred pity for my aunt, who all these years had had nothing except that child-like creature there before the TV set, and who might not have even him much longer.

"Yes," I said.

"You knew this last night?"

"Yes."

"Why didn't you tell me?"

"Because I'd promised Philip not to. Besides—" I broke off.

"You thought I might warn Eric?"

I nodded.

"I might have," she said dully. "I suppose I'd have done anything to keep from being separated from Byron."

I whispered, "Oh, I'm so sorry, so sorry!"

"None of it's your fault," she said, in that dull voice. "Anyway, it was bound to happen sometime." She paused. "Could you eat something?"

I shook my head. "I just want to stay here by the phone." Pulling out the straight chair beside the phone table, I sat down.

"I'm not hungry either. If you want me to, I'll wait here with you. I've already given Byron his dinner."

"Yes, please wait with me."

She touched a wall switch, and the overhead light came on. I watched her walk down the hall and through the living room doorway. When she came back a few minutes later, she was carrying a small wooden folding chair in one hand, and her mending basket in the other.

By the time the grandfather's clock gave a preliminary whir, and then began to strike the hour of eight, I felt that we'd been sitting there beside the phone for at least a week. Neither of us had talked much. She asked me how and why Philip had tracked Eric Hauklid down, and I'd told her. After that she sewed in silence. At last, feeling that I'd go mad if I just sat there staring at the minute hand of the clock, I asked her to give me something to mend. She handed me a blue kitchen apron with an unraveled hem.

Now, as the clock began to strike the hour, I dropped the apron into her sewing basket, and then placed my hand on the table, inches from the phone. The clock's last stroke was still vibrating when the phone rang. I snatched it up. "Hello?"

"Hello, Catherine," Eric Hauklid's calm voice said.

"Please," I said, "please—"

"Will you meet me in half an hour?"

"Oh, yes, yes! Where?"

"There's a summerhouse in the woods, about a mile from where you are now. Maybe you've noticed car tracks branching off the private road? They're on your left as you drive toward the highway."

"I've seen them."

"Don't turn onto the tracks. Leave your car on the road and come to the summerhouse on foot."

"Yes. Let me speak to her. Please, please!"

"I can't. I left her in the summerhouse while I came to phone you."

He must be in that phone booth on the highway, I realized, the one near the field the circus had rented.

"I assure you she's all right," he went on. "I've had to bind and gag her, but she's all right."

Nicole, lying alone in that dark little house deep in the woods, hearing the night sounds, and unable even to scream out her terror—

"Be there precisely at eighty-thirty. No sooner. And come alone."

"Yes. Oh, God, yes."

He hung up.

My hand was shaking so hard that when I tried to replace the phone, it missed the cradle and clattered on the table's surface. My aunt picked it up and put it in place. "When?" she asked.

"Eight-thirty. The summerhouse." I stood up. My legs

were trembling, but I'd be able to make it up the stairs, get my handbag. "I'm leaving right now."

"But it won't take you more than a few minutes to—"

"The car might stall or something, and make me late. I'll drive to the tracks leading to the summerhouse, and then wait until it's time to walk the rest of the way."

Only minutes later, I left the house and crossed the still-muddy yard. Dimly I was aware of a first-quarter moon in a cloudless sky. Getting into my car, I finally managed to insert the ignition key. The engine caught. I turned, and drove into the road's leafy tunnel. I took the first curve—and then jammed on the brake.

Philip Owen, his thin face determined, stood directly in the path of my headlights.

19

Even before my car came to a full stop, he was running toward it. He jerked the door open and slid onto the seat beside me.

"Get out!" I said, in a strangled voice. "Oh, God! You're going to ruin everything!"

"Catherine!"

With both hands, I shoved at his arm and shoulder. "Get out! Get clear away from here!"

He caught both my wrists. "Now listen to me."

Struggling to free myself, I cried, "He's less than a mile from here! And I told him I'd come there alone!" With heightened fear, I realized that my voice had risen on those last words. Sounds carry far in the country, especially on a still night. I whispered hoarsely, "Where's your car?"

"I left it over on the highway, and cut through the woods to wait for you."

His hold had slackened a little. Jerking my wrists free, I said, "I told you not to come near me. Now go!" Fingers curled, I tried to reach his face with my nails.

He slapped me.

As I stared at him, my ears ringing, he gathered me against his shoulder. "Oh, darling, darling! I had to. You wouldn't listen. Listen to me now, Catherine. I could tell when you phoned that you were in no condition to think straight. I had to think for you."

Rigid in his arms, I said nothing.

"Don't you see? He believes that no one except you and that poor aunt of yours know who he is. He figures that whatever has kept her silent all these years will go on doing that. So that leaves just you. Do you understand?"

Really listening now, I nodded.

"If you go alone to that meeting place— Where is it?"

"A summerhouse. About a mile ahead, there are car tracks leading to it.'

"I've seen it. It's in a clearing, isn't it, with one set of tracks leading toward this road, and another set leading in the opposite direction?"

I nodded.

"If you go there alone, you'll find Nicole alive, all right. He must be planning to question you until he's sure that except for your aunt, you're the only one who knows. Then he'll kill you, and probably Nicole, too."

He was right. Cold and numb and speechless in the circle of his arms, I knew he was right.

"Maybe he plans to run after that. Or maybe—since by now he must consider himself some sort of Nietzschean superman—he plans to hide your bodies, and go back to the farmhouse, and make your aunt give out the story that you suddenly decided to go back to Chicago."

With lips that felt wooden, I asked, "But if I told him that you knew who he was, and had even found my uncle's body—"

"He'd just shoot you, and make a run for it. Why not? He'd get a head start that way. And if he got caught—well, the penalty for three murders is the same as for one."

Again I moved my numb lips. "What can we do?" My eyes flew to the dashboard clock. Fourteen minutes after eight. "If I'm not there by eight-thirty, he might— Oh, God! He might—"

His arms tightened around me. "Yes, he might, if you're quite a bit late. He might conclude you'd told the police. He'd run. And he wouldn't want her to be able to tell what clothing he wore, or in which direction he'd driven out of the clearing."

Despite his encircling arms, my whole body trembled. "There isn't time to call the police—"

"No. I'd have called them before this, if I'd known where to send them. But you were right when you said over the phone that he might be somewhere close by. I didn't dare send them to the house, or even go there myself. And if I'd phoned you, you'd just have screamed at me, and hung up."

I was screaming now, but silently, inside myself. "Then how—?"

"I'll get out now, and crouch down in the back seat. You drive to the summerhouse. Go inside. In about one minute, I'll follow you."

"But if he has a gun—"

"I have, too. And his won't be out in the open. He'll have it inside his jacket, or perhaps in a drawer, until he's ready to use it. But mine will be right in my hand."

"You're—you're going to kill him?"

"Not unless I have to. I'd rather hold the gun on him, while you go for the police. I want him to feel what my father felt when those German soldiers—" Breaking off, he opened the car door.

I cried, in sudden recollection, "He told me not to drive into the clearing!"

"We'll have to. There isn't time to make it now, if we go part of the way on foot. And you mustn't be too late."

I looked at the clock, and saw with a terrible throb of my heart that it was nineteen minutes past eight.

He got into the back seat. I put the car in gear. He said, leaning forward to cross his arms on the back of the front seat, "Drive carefully. The leaves in the road are still slippery from yesterday. He won't get the wind up if you're only a few minutes late. But if you slide into a tree, or get bogged down—"

I did drive carefully, sweat-soaked hands gripping the wheel, eyes leaving the tortuous, leaf-filled ruts for an instant every now and then to look at the dashboard clock.

It was eight thirty-one when I turned onto the tracks branching off to the left.

Philip whispered, "Don't worry. You're almost there." He said nothing after that. A glance into the rear-view mirror showed me an apparently empty back seat.

After perhaps a minute, the broad-leaved trees bordering the track gave way to pitch pine. No layers of leaves now between my tires and the mud. Just pine needles, and potholes where water still stood. Again and again as I drove across those potholes, I expected my wheels to lose traction, but they didn't.

I turned a slight curve, and again felt that painful leap of my heart. For about twenty feet ahead, glistening black water filled the tracks. Instinct made me step hard on the accelerator. If I went through fast enough, and if the layer of pine needles beneath the water was thick enough—

A sheet of water struck my windshield. I plowed on. The water became shallower. Only a few feet more now. Ahead was a dry stretch, pitted with potholes, and then the moonlit clearing.

As the car moved onto dry ground, I glanced at the clock. Eight thirty-six. Speeding up, I bumped over the potholes and into the clearing.

Too late, I saw it was a sea of mud, glimmering in the

moonlight. The tires slewed sickeningly, and I heard a rear door bang against the side of the car. As I fought the wheel, I looked toward the dark bulk of the summer-house. A tall man stood in the doorway.

The car stopped skidding. I switched off the ignition, got out onto the muddy ground.

Perhaps he'd caught a glimpse of Philip's crouched figure when the door flew open. Perhaps, because I'd disobeyed his instructions not to drive into the clearing, he thought that the police might be following close behind me. Whatever the reason, he must have realized his danger, because now the doorway was empty.

I heard a rasping sound, and knew he must be raising a screen of the eight-sided structure. Then I saw him, a dark, bent figure, running at an angle into the woods. He carried something in his arms.

From the corner of my eye I saw a dull metallic gleam. Whirling, I found that Philip stood beside the car. The gun in his hand was leveled at that running figure.

I struck his arm up. "Don't!" I screamed. "He's got Nicole."

20

With my feet threatening to slide from under me at each step, I ran across the muddy clearing toward the point where that bent figure had disappeared into the woods. A flashlight's beam shot past me, illuminating the dark bulk of the Hauklids' old sedan and, beside it, the entrance to a narrow path through the trees.

Philip caught up with me when I was less than a yard from the path's entrance. "I'll go ahead." As he plunged past me, I saw that his right hand still held the gun.

Although slippery with pine needles, the path was firm underfoot. Within seconds, Philip was yards ahead of me. I ran on, eyes fixed on the thin figure silhouetted against the flashlight's glow, and scarcely noticing when branches whipped across my body or my face.

We turned a curve in the path, then another. At the third turn, I almost ran into Philip. He'd stopped short, and was playing the flashlight's beam on the surrounding tree trunks. He whispered, "The path just peters out here."

That circling beam of light found something, paused for an instant, and then swept on. But I'd seen it, a rectangular, freshly dug hole, only a yard or so from where we stood. So, I thought, fighting off the faintness that threatened to overwhelm me, Philip had been right. Hauklid had intended that my daughter and I would never leave these woods.

Philip said, in a low voice, "I'm just going to plunge straight ahead through the trees. You'd better wait here. Huddle as close to a tree trunk as you can, and keep quiet. Even if he doubles back this way, there's little chance he'll see you."

"No! I've got to try to keep up with you. I couldn't wait here, imagining—"

For an instant he studied my face in the flashlight's refracted glow. Perhaps my expression told him that I'd seen that rectangle of freshly dug earth, because he said abruptly, "All right." Turning, he moved away between two pine trunks. I followed as best I could, unable to see him now and then as he threaded his way through the trees, but never losing sight of the flashlight's glow.

Suddenly I froze. A moaning sound had come from somewhere among the trees to my right. It had sounded like a man, thank God, not a child. I called, in a strained whisper, "Philip!"

Branches crackled and twigs snapped as he made his way back to me. I whispered, "Someone, over there—"

Moving cautiously, he took the direction I'd indicated. After a moment he called softly, "Catherine."

Pointing the flashlight downward, he swung it around to light my way through the tree trunks. I halted beside him.

A man I'd never seen before lay prone in the flashlight's glow, the left side of his face resting on the leaf-strewn ground. Of almost skeletal thinness, he wore trousers that had once been part of someone's cheap blue suit, and a ragged striped jersey. The visible side of his face was a grotesque half mask—the cheek painted a dead-white, with red paint superimposed to create the clown's traditional down-turned mouth. A foot or so from his outstretched right hand, a green bottle that once must have held wine or cheap brandy glittered in the light.

"Take this," Philip said, and handed me the gun. Dropping to one knee, he directed the flashlight onto the back of the man's head. At the same time, with the fingers of his left hand, he felt for the pulse in the thin wrist. "He's been slugged, and only minutes ago. The blood's still running. He's alive, though."

I whispered, "He must be one of the roustabouts from that circus across the highway. But I thought they wore clown suits."

"They do. His suit's on Hauklid." He stood up and took the gun from my hand. "Come on."

I followed him as, angling toward the highway, he threaded his way through the trees. In my effort to keep up, I often ran into low branches, and once I banged my left shoulder against a tree trunk, but I was only dimly conscious of pain. Soon we began to hear band music. It grew louder as we hurried through the trees.

We emerged onto the highway. On its opposite side, bright arc lights had been trained on a big brown tent, from whose open doorway brassy music spilled. To the left of the tent stretched a dark field, but the field on its right was filled with parked cars. Other cars had been parked on both sides of the highway.

Running, we crossed the road. Animal cages and brightly painted circus wagons stood at haphazard angles in the space between the highway and the tent, but a broad aisle leading to the ticket booth beside the tent entrance had been left clear. We hurried toward the booth. A short, heavy-set man stood beside it, talking to the woman ticket seller.

When we reached him, Philip asked, "Have you see a stranger around here? Tall man in a roustabout's outfit?"

The man was staring at us with alarmed disfavor. I became aware that Philip—trouser legs muddy, dark nylon jacket ripped, cheek scratched and bleeding—looked far from presentable, and that I probably looked even worse. The man said coldly, "Why do you ask?" He added, "I'm the manager."

I cried, "Please! He kidnaped my little girl."

Instantly the manager's face altered. Before he could speak, Philip said, "We found one of your roustabouts in the woods. He'd been slugged and stripped of his clown suit. So we—"

The manager didn't wait to hear the rest. "Danny!" he shouted.

A thin man of about forty emerged from between two of the nearby circus wagons. The manager said, "You see a new roustabout around here tonight?"

"Sure. Didn't you hire him? Real tall fellow, sort of yellow-gray hair?

The manager asked sharply, "Where is he now?"

"Why, in the main tent. He didn't have makeup on, so I took him into the makeup wagon and slapped grease paint on him. Then he went into the tent. That was—oh, five minutes ago."

I asked tautly, "Did he have a little girl with him?"

Danny stared at me. "Hell no, lady."

Then he'd left her there, someplace in the woods. Whirling, I ran back toward the highway. Philip shouted my name, but I didn't stop.

It was another sound that stopped me. A kind of strangled whimper from one of the animal cages somewhere to my right. I called "Nicole!" and the sound was repeated. Heart thudding with hope, I darted past a red and gold circus wagon, and stopped before a wheeled animal cage.

For an instant I thought the cage was empty. Then I saw, back in one corner, the gleam of pale hair, and the faint luminosity of brown eyes wide with fear above the cloth that bound her mouth.

I remember trying to slide the barred door aside. I don't remember crying out, but I must have, because suddenly there were people around me. Someone, probably Danny, slid the door open and reached inside.

I held her tightly in my arms while Philip untied strips of blue cloth that bound her wrists and ankles, and the white strip, probably part of a man's nylon muffler, that covered her mouth. The wail that burst from her made me feel faint with relief. She sounded frightened, my little girl, and furious as the traditional wet hen. But surely those healthy bellows meant that she was otherwise all right.

I soothed her with kisses and murmurs. After a moment her wails quieted to indignant sobs. I said, "Did he hurt you, darling?"

Her voice was thick with tears and rage. "He tied up my mouth, and he took me away, and he ran with me through the woods."

Thank God. Apparently it had been no worse than that.

Her arms tightened around my neck. "He's a bad man," she announced loudly.

"Yes, darling," I said, and became aware that Philip and the other men had gone. The only person standing beside me now was an enormously fat woman in a red-spangled dress and theatrical makeup. Like a twin waterfall, a necklace of false pearls as big as marbles jutted out over the cliff of her bosom and plunged toward her nonexistent waist. She was saying things like, "Oh, the poor little darling," and, to me, "What happened, dearie? What happened?"

Still stroking my daughter's hair, I stared at the entrance to the tent. The lights inside it were different now. Some had been dimmed, so that a cone of white glare falling from somewhere at the top of the tent looked all the brighter.

Philip in there, looking for Eric Hauklid. But it was almost certain that Hauklid, one of a dozen or so in clowns' costumes, his face hidden by a painted mask, would spot his hunter before Philip recognized him.

I stood there, frightened and helpless, with my now quietly sniffling child in my arms, and the fat lady asking questions. I noticed fleetingly that Nicole, even while she made those aggrieved noises, was looking at the fat lady with admiring interest.

Another voice said, "Cathy! What happened to you?" I looked up into the bony, horrified face of that old circus buff, my employer.

I said tautly, "Steve, will you—" Breaking off, I looked down at Nicole. "Darling, this is the nice man who gave Mama her job. Will you stay with him for a few minutes?"

Nicole stared at him doubtfully. His expression was equally dubious. "Damn it, Cathy, I came to see the circus, and I've missed a third of it already. Besides, I don't know anything about kids."

"I'll take her," the fat lady said. The look she gave Steve was heavy with scorn for all men. She reached out red-spangled arms to Nicole. "Come to Eloise, sweetheart."

My daughter hiccuped, smiled, and allowed herself to be gathered to that enormous bosom. The woman carried her to the red and gold circus wagon and sat down on its step. I said to Steve, "Please! You stay with her, too. I'll feel better if you do."

"Cathy, you look like a sparrow that's been caught in a badminton game. Will you please—"

"Hauklid kidnaped her. He's somewhere in the tent now, and Philip's after him."

His face changed. He asked no more questions. "Don't worry. I won't stir a step away from her," he said, and walked toward the two seated on the circus wagon step. Turning, I moved quickly toward the tent. The woman in the ticket booth didn't challenge me as I walked past her and slipped inside the entrance. I halted, looking around.

From the top of the tent, arc lamps threw brilliant light on the ring, where, with much cracking of a long whip, a husky woman in a scarlet lion tamer's costume was putting three elderly looking tigers through their paces. The rest of the tent was in comparative shadow. But I could see the attentive faces of spectators in the stands, and the figures moving along the tanbark path that encircled the ring—popcorn venders in white coats, and roustabouts in sleazy yellow clown costumes, their grease-painted faces topped by pointed yellow caps. Some of them were moving equipment—a trampoline, an enormous drum, a low trapeze—that apparently were to be used in the next act. Others lounged against the barricade that separated the spectators from the tanbark.

My gaze flew from one clown-costumed figure to another. Most of them were too short. But there were a few tall ones. Could he be that one wheeling a trapeze toward the center ring? Or that one clear at the other side of the tent, standing between the band platform and the exit directly opposite me? Or that man on the right side of the tent, lounging with elbows propped on the barricade?

My gaze, traveling full circle, found Philip. He stood not ten feet away, on the other side of the entrance. His gaze, too, was moving from one costumed figure to another. And then, just as I was about to call to him in a whisper, he turned, moved past me, and walked swiftly and purposively along the tanbark toward that exit on the other side of the tent.

All the lights came on. Even though my attention was concentrated on Philip, I was aware of applause, and of the animal trainer cracking her whip as the tigers leaped into their cage. Then I realized Philip's objective—the tall man in clown costume who stood beside the band platform.

I saw the roustabout's right hand, at chest level, dive inside that loose costume. It came out with something that gleamed in the brilliant light. There was a sharp crack, and the ringing impact of a bullet against one of the metal poles that supported the tent. A split second later there was another shot. A section of canvas just above the roustabout's head billowed outward. Whirling, he ran out into the darkness.

People had begun to scream. The band, evidently hoping to prevent panic, had struck up "Beer Barrel Polka." But it was no use. The spectators, many of them carrying children or leading them by the hand, hurried down from the tiers of seats and streamed past me as I stood there, momentarily paralyzed. Through the babble of voices, and the band's blaring music, I heard four shots in quick succession from somewhere out in the darkness.

With a leap of anguished terror, I realized that Hauklid would have had the advantage. To him, already in darkness, Philip would have been a clear target as he ran from the lighted tent.

I found I could move. Shoving at shoulders and arms, I made my way against the current, past the still-playing musicians, out into the night.

Ahead of me stretched the plowed contours of a newly harvested potato field. I saw that several people, braver or more curious than those shoving their way out of the tent's other opening, had preceded me. They'd gathered in a motionless and silent group about twenty yards away.

With my feet sinking into the soft damp earth, I ran toward them. "Please," I said to someone's back. The man let me through. "Please," I repeated to someone else. He moved aside, and I was in the circle's cleared center.

By the glow of several flashlights, I saw Hauklid lying on the ground. Blood stained the chest of his sleazy costume. More blood had streamed from the left side of his head down his painted cheek. Philip knelt on one knee beside him. The wounded man, his voice labored and urgent, was speaking what I knew must be Norwegian. In the same language, Philip asked what sounded like a question.

I dropped to my knees. "You're all right?"

Shooting me a side glance, Philip nodded. Then he returned his gaze to that painted white face, rendered doubly grotesque by the blood streaming down one side of it. Hauklid was still speaking in that breathy, earnest voice. His hand reached up to grasp Philip's arm, as if for emphasis. He spoke a few more words, in a voice that had faded to a hoarse whisper. Then his eyes, so remarkably blue against the white grease paint, glazed over. His hand slid from Philip's arm to lie on the loose soil.

Philip stood up. A voice said authoritatively, from outside the circle of silent spectators, "Let me through, please. I'm a doctor."

A portly man with rimless glasses stepped into the circle of light. In his hand was a black satchel. Philip said, "I'm sure he's gone. I don't think you could have saved him."

The doctor asked sharply, "You're the one who shot this man?"

"He shot first. Several hundred witnesses can testify to that."

Taking my arm, Philip drew me to my feet. Somewhere in the distance, sirens wailed. The crowd, larger now, fell back to let us through.

A moment later I said, in a shaken voice, "I was so afraid. I mean, when you ran after him, you had the light behind you—"

"He didn't take advantage of it fast enough. Too busy looking for some kind of cover, probably. And after a few seconds, the advantage was all the other way. In that light yellow costume and white grease paint, he was a clear target."

I stumbled in the soft soil, and Philip caught my elbow. I said, "What was he saying?"

"His mind was wandering. He'd gone back about thirty years. Maybe because I answered him in Norwegian, he thought I was one of his old Nazi pals."

"But what—"

"He was exhorting me to keep on looking for something he lost in the swamp. It's a lead box, I gathered, and it holds a list of locations of arms depots."

"Arms depots!"

"Places where Nazi sympathizers in this country were supposed to have hidden arms before and during the war. I'll report it, of course, but I doubt if the government will be much interested. My impression is that years and years ago internal security men rounded up many such weapons, and the people who'd collected them. I don't imagine that they'll go to much trouble, at this late date, to find out whether or not they missed a few."

I thought of Hauklid, spending those self-imprisoned decades in that isolated farmhouse. And all because he considered himself the custodian of that leaden box.

I cried, "Why? Why did he think that box was important?"

"Not primarily for the list of arms depots, I imagine.

Undoubtedly he knew that most of the arms would be useless after all these years. No, what was important to him must have been the names of the people who collected those arms. He thought they'd become the leaders when his kind takes over, in one guise or another."

I recalled what my aunt had said. "You mean," I asked, half incredulously, "that he was hoping for an American Hitler?"

"Not hoping. Expecting. It's the delusion such men have. They can't believe people really mean that stuff about liberty and justice for all. A man like that thinks that everyone, underneath, is an Eric Hauklid."

Ahead of us, light spilled from the tent doorway through which Hauklid had dashed only minutes ago. "Maybe he was right about some of us," Philip said, "but not most. I'm sure of that."

We moved into the tent, past the now-empty bandstand. Roustabouts were clearing away the wooden tubs and hoops used in the animal act, and the trampoline and trapeze for the act that was supposed to have followed. Just the sight of those glistening, dead-white faces, most of them set with the quietly suffering eyes of the alcoholic, made my nerves tighten with remembered terror.

Philip asked, "Where did you leave Nicole?"

"Out by one of the circus wagons. Steve Connery's with her, and one of the women performers."

"I'll have to wait here for the police. Steve can drive you and Nicole home."

Home. As of right now, home was that rundown farmhouse where my aunt waited in quiet resignation.

I stopped and faced him. "Will Aunt Marian have to stand trial?"

"I doubt it, especially now that Hauklid's dead. It was through that retarded son of hers that he kept his hold over her, wasn't it?"

I nodded. "She was afraid that if Hauklid were arrested, she'd be too, and then Byron would be placed in an institution."

He said, as we moved forward again, "Well, grand juries are made up of people, not machines. I doubt that any group of men and women will indict her. They'll feel she's been punished far too much already."

We emerged through the tent's other opening. True to their trust, Steve and the lady in red still waited with Nicole beside the circus wagon. All three were standing. My daughter, with that string of fake pearls now dangling from her neck to below her knees, chattered to the woman in a high, clear voice.

She caught sight of Philip and me. Racing toward us, with the pearls bouncing against her legs at each step, she held up her arms to me. Her face wore that babyish expression it always does when she decides it would be pleasant to be treated again like a two-year-old.

I bent, intending to lift her into my arms, but Philip said, "You're a big girl, Nicole, and your mother is tired. Why don't you walk between us?"

I straightened. The brook-brown eyes looked up limpidly at Philip. "Will we have a beach dinner?"

"Yes." He turned his smiling gaze toward me for a long moment, and then looked down at my daughter, "If I get my way, we'll be having beach dinners for years and years."

"Then I'll walk," my little horse trader said.

Each of us clasping one of Nicole's hands, we moved toward Steve and the resplendent fat lady.